CHEERS

A Guide to Drinking in New York

Sandy Stern

AN OWL BOOK
_____

HENRY HOLT and COMPANY
NEW YORK

Published by Henry Holt and Company, Inc.,
115 West 18th Street, New York, New York 10011.
Published in Canada by Fitzhenry & Whiteside Limited,
195 Allstate Parkway, Markham, Ontario L3R 4T8.

Library of Congress Cataloging-in-Publication Data
Stern, Sandy.
Cheers: a guide to drinking in New York / by Sandy Stern.
        p.   cm.
"An Owl book."
ISBN 0-8050-0676-1 (pbk.)
1. Hotels, taverns, etc.—New York (N.Y.)—Guide-books.
2. New York (N.Y.)—Description—1981–   —Guide-books.
I. Title.
TX950.53.S74 1988
647′.95′7471—dc 19   87-30972
                                                 CIP

First Edition

Designed by Robert Bull Design
Printed in the United States of America
1 3 5 7 9 10 8 6 4 2

ISBN 0-8050-0676-1

CONTENTS

Like a good toast:
I would like to thank
Kelly Mauldin Harrell, for her editorial assistance;
Stanley J. Zielin, for his imbibing camaraderie;
and to Mom, I toast you in the sky.

INTRODUCTION

New York City is the greatest city in the world. If you are a native, you automatically agree. If you have relocated, chances are you agree too. And if you are here visiting—welcome. I suspect in no time you will agree as well.

This city offers more choices and opportunities to try, to have, to do, to feel, to see, in any one place at any given time than anywhere else in the country. Undeniably fast-paced and fun, New York is filled with some of the most successful, creative, and spirited people in the world. Those of us who have decided to live here, and those just on a quick visit, have all been drawn here to take advantage of the incredible opportunities and options. Whether you are a New Yorker living and breathing a seven-day work week, or simply in for a blowout holiday, all of us seem to enjoy and partake in the Gotham scene, which includes dining, drinking, and desserting.

As a born-and-bred die-hard New Yorker, I have realized how meeting someone for a drink has become fundamental to our existence in this town and how easily it can enhance the New York experience in an affordable and accessible way. Clearly restaurants play an integral role in our lives, whether it be socially or professionally. The "dining-out going-out" industry has been elevated to a level approaching art—or at least to center stage. Few argue its theatricality. The weekly *New York Times* reviews by Bryan Miller, following in the footsteps of Mimi Sheraton and Marion Burros, eagerly awaited and read as familiarly as Vincent Canby; magazines focusing on food and restaurants enjoying huge subscription audiences; and the multitude of restaurant guidebooks on the market attest to dining out as something of a national pastime; and if you magnify that ten times over, you have New York. And when we frame dinner with cocktails and nightcaps, the "let's meet for drinks" phenomenon certainly rivals

1

the flourishing restaurant scene. For those who cannot afford astronomically priced dinners, meeting for drinks has become the easy front-runner. And from the looks of it, drinking is here to stay.

How many times have we started (or ended) a conversation with "Let's get together and meet for a drink," to have it finished with a "Great idea—let's—but *where* should we go?" New York is undeniably a city of neighborhoods, and although each of us is in love with our own neighborhood, we enjoy venturing out. Often, however, one can be left feeling like a stranger in a strange land. With what New York has to offer in terms of drinking options, I cannot think of a more appropriate vehicle for easing this process than this guide to drinking in New York.

How many times do you want to find a romantic bar located in the Village that attracts a popular and comfortable after-work crowd? What would be the perfect bar to bring Aunt Tillie to before she returns home to Tucson? By using the cross-referenced bar listings on the following pages, you should be able to find a bar tailor-made to fit your specifications. But beware. Equally interesting and relevant to New York life is the pace, trendiness, and chameleonlike character of its clubs. I can safely say that, at the time of this writing, the reviews accurately capture and reflect the spirit, crowd, and ambiance of the establishments. But as Dorothy said in *The Wizard of Oz*, "How things come and go so quickly around here!" Little did she know how relevant her statement was to the nature of New York nightlife. Keep in mind: places change, names change, whole bars will come and go—some churches will become bars, and some bars will become churches. Personalities of bars change as well. Some change over the course of a day. Some overnight. Some over time. I apologize if I did not know that a typical East Side neighborhood bar closes its doors at seven P.M. and metamorphoses into a West Side sex club three hours later. If my review is totally off base, I apologize for any inconvenience, and offer you a drink—on me. As a rule, call first and make sure you are going to the right place.

I have included a lot of bars. I do not, and cannot, lay claim to having reviewed every single bar in New York. Not only would my liver have walked out, but my strength and perseverance would have been left somewhere in the gutter. Although there will always be "one more bar" to review, I am quite sure that you will find the following compilation extensive. If I did forget your favorite corner neighborhood bar, however, I humbly apologize. But take solace in knowing that it will remain anonymous.

Finally, I do not think any book reviewing drinking in New York can be written or read with a whole lot of sobriety. Therefore I have used the following Martini System for rating each of the establishments. A four-martini bar is hard to beat. Use it as a guide, or use it as a laugh. I am using it as just another vehicle to communicate my subjective opinions. So enjoy it. Find a new spot. Try a new drink. Meet a new friend. And, cheers.

BARS BY LOCATION

BELOW HOUSTON

Barocco, 301 Church Street, 431-1445
Capsuoto Frères, 451 Washington Street, 966-4900
Delmonico's, 56 Beaver Street, 422-4747
√ **Ear Inn,** 326 Spring Street, 226-9060
Fanelli's Cafe, 94 Prince Street, 226-9412
Greene Street Cafe, 101 Greene Street, 925-2415
Harry's at Hanover Square, 1 Hanover Square, 425-3412
Heartbreak, 179 Varick Street, 691-2388
√ **How's Bayou Cafe,** 355 Greenwich Street, 925-5405
I Tre Merli Inc., 463 West Broadway, 254-8699
La Gamelle, 58 Grand Street, 431-6695
The New Deal, 152 Spring Street, 431-3663
North River Bar, 145 Hudson Street, 226-9411
The Odeon, 145 West Broadway, 233-0507
Prince Street Bar & Restaurant, 125 Prince Street,
  228-8130
Provence, 38 MacDougal Street, 475-7500
Puffy's, 81 Hudson Street, 766-9159
Raoul's, 180 Prince Street, 674-0708
River Cafe, 1 Water Street, Brooklyn Heights,
  718-522-5200
Riverrun Cafe, 176 Franklin Street, 966-3894
Smoke Stacks Lightning, 380 Canal Street, 226-0485
S.O.B.'s, 204 Varick Street, 243-4940
The Soho Kitchen and Bar, 130 Greene Street, 925-1866
√ **South Street Seaport,** Water & Fulton Streets, 732-7678
√ **Sporting Club,** 99 Hudson Street, 219-0900
Tapis Rouge, 157 Duane Street, 732-5555
Two Eleven Bar & Restaurant, 211 West Broadway,
  925-7202
J. S. VanDam, 150 Varick Street, 929-7466

Windows on the World, 1 World Trade Center, 938-1111
Wine Bar, 422 West Broadway, 431-4790

HOUSTON TO 14TH STREET

Art Cafe, 151 Second Avenue, 598-0366
Arthur's Tavern, 57 Grove Street, 675-6879
Automatic Slims, 733 Washington Street, 645-8660
Bandito West, 33 Greenwich Avenue, 807-0120
The Bar, Second Avenue and 4th Street, no phone
  number
Bar Lui, 625 Broadway, 473-8787
Bayamo, 705 Broadway, 475-5151
Big Kahuna, 622 Broadway, 460-9633
The Blue Mill Tavern, 50 Commerce Street, 243-7114
Boy Bar, 15 St. Mark's Place, 674-9219
Bradley's Restaurant, 70 University Place, 228-6440,
  473-9700
Bruxelles, 118 Greenwich Avenue, 206-1830
Caliente Cab Company, 61 Seventh Avenue South,
  243-8517
Caramba!!, 684 Broadway, 420-9817
Chapiteau Restaurant, 105 West 13th Street, 929-8833
Chez Ma Tante, 189 West 10th Street, 620-0223
Chumley's, 86 Bedford Street, 675-4449
Covent Gardens, 133 West 13th Street, 675-0020
The Cubbyhole, 438 Hudson Street, 243-9079
Jimmy Day's, 186 West 4th Street, 929-8942
Dukie's, 345 East 9th Street, no phone number
Duplex, 55 Grove Street, 255-5438
Five Oaks, 49 Grove Street, 243-8885
Florent, 69 Gansevoort Street, 989-5779
Formerly Joe's, 230 West 4th Street, 242-9100
Frank's, 431 West 14th Street, 243-1349
Gotham Bar and Grill, 12 East 12th Street, 620-4020
Great Jones Cafe, 54 Great Jones Street, 674-9304
The Grove Club, 70 Grove Street, 242-1408

Holiday Cocktail Lounge & Restaurant, 75 St. Mark's
  Place, 777-9637
Indochine, 430 Lafayette Street, 505-5111
Julius, 159 West 10th Street, 929-9672
Kingfisher, 644 Broadway, 673-6480
King Tut's Wah Wah Hut, 112 Avenue A, 254-7772
The Lion's Head, 59 Christopher Street, 929-0670
Dan Lynch Bar and Restaurant, 221 Second Avenue,
  677-0911
Marie's Crisis, 59 Grove Street, 243-9323
McSorley's Old Ale House, 15 East 7th Street, 473-8800
The Milk Bar, 22 Seventh Avenue South, 675-4631
Miracles, 46 Greenwich Avenue, 691-1636
Night Birds Restaurant & Bar, 92 Second Avenue, 254-4747
One Fifth, 1 Fifth Avenue, 260-3434
One If by Land, 17 Barrow Street, 228-0822 *7AV – W4 ST*
Rectangles, 159 Second Avenue, 677-8410
Riviera Cafe, 225 West 4th Street, 242-8732
Siberia, 804 Washington Street, 463-8521
Sunset Strip, 95 Horatio Street, 645-0808
Tortilla Flats, 767 Washington Street, 243-1053
Uncle Charlie's Downtown, 56 Greenwich Avenue,
  255-8787
Vazac's, 108 Avenue B, 473-8840
West 4th Street Saloon, 174 West 4th Street, 255-0518
The White Horse Tavern, 567 Hudson Street, 243-9260
Woody's, 140 Seventh Avenue South, 242-1200
The World, 2nd Street and Avenue C, 477-8677

14TH TO 34TH STREET

America, 9 East 18th Street, 505-2110
The Ballroom, 253 West 28th Street, 244-3005
Cadillac Bar, 15 West 21st Street, 645-7220
Cafe Society, 915 Broadway, 529-8282
Chelsea Place, 147 Eighth Avenue, 924-8413
Chevys, 27 West 20th Street, 924-0205

Claire Restaurant, 156 Seventh Avenue, 255-1955
The Eagle's Nest, 142 Eleventh Avenue, 691-8451
Empire Diner, 210 Tenth Avenue, 243-2736
Greensleeves, 543 Second Avenue, 725-9383
Harvey's Chelsea Restaurant, 108 West 18th Street, 243-5644
Il Palazzo, 18 West 18th Street, 924-3800
Limelight, 47 West 20th Street, 807-7850
Lola, 30 West 22nd Street, 675-6700
Man Ray Bistro, 169 Eighth Avenue, 627-4220
Metropolis Cafe, 31 Union Square West, 675-2300
Mumbles, 603 Second Avenue, 889-0750
Nell's, 246 West 14th Street, 675-1567
Old Town Bar & Restaurant, 45 East 18th Street, 473-8874
Palladium, 126 East 14th Street, 473-7171
Pete's Tavern, 129 East 18th Street, 473-7676
Private Eyes Inc., 12 West 21st Street, 206-7770
Quatorze, 240 West 14th Street, 206-7006
Rick's 181 Lounge, 181 Eighth Avenue, 691-9845
Savage, 208 West 23rd Street, 691-4421
Shelter, 540 Second Avenue, 684-4207
Sofi, 102 Fifth Avenue, 463-8888
Stringfellows, 35 East 21st Street, 254-2444
1018, 515 West 18th Street, 645-5156
Tunnel, 220 12th Avenue, 529-6324
23rd Street Bar & Grill, 158 East 23rd Street, 533-8877
Twenty Twenty, 20 West 20th Street, 627-1444
Union Square Cafe, 21 East 16th Street, 243-4020
Water Club, 500 East 30th Street, 683-3333
Zig Zag, 206 West 23rd Street, 645-5060

34TH TO 59TH STREET
(West of Fifth Avenue)

Algonquin Hotel, Algonquin Hotel Lounge, 59 West 44th Street, 840-6800
Joe Allen, 326 West 46th Street, 581-6464

Barrymore's, 267 West 45th Street, 541-4500
Bellini, 777 Seventh Avenue, 265-7770
Between the Bread, 145 West 55th Street, 581-1189
Cafe de la Paix (*see* St. Moritz Hotel), 50 Central Park South, 755-5800
Cafe 43, 147 West 43rd Street, 869-4200
Cafe Madeleine, 405 West 43rd Street, 246-2993
Caramba! 918 Eighth Avenue, 245-7910
Century Cafe, 132 West 43rd Street, 398-1988
China Grill, 60 West 53rd Street, 333-7788
Curtain Up! 402 West 43rd Street, 546-7272
Don't Tell Mama, 343 West 46th Street, 757-0788
4D, 610 West 56th Street, 247-0612
Hard Rock Cafe, 221 West 57th Street, 489-6565
The Improvisation, 358 West 44th Street, 765-8268
Jezebel, 630 Ninth Avenue, 582-1045
The Landmark Tavern, 626 Eleventh Avenue, 757-8595
Lavin's, 23 West 39th Street, 921-1288
Marriott Marquis Hotel, Broadway Lounge, JW's, and The View Bar, 1535 Broadway, 398-1900
Mike's American Bar & Grill, 650 Tenth Avenue, 246-4115
Novotel, Novotel Wine Bistro, 226 West 52nd Street, 315-0100
The Oak Bar (*see* Plaza Hotel), Fifth Avenue at 59th Street, 759-3000
O'Neals, 60 West 57th Street, 399-2361
Oyster Bar at the Plaza (*see* Plaza Hotel), Fifth Avenue at 59th Street, 759-3000
Palio, 151 West 51st Street, 245-4850
Parker Meridien Hotel, Bar Montparnasse, 118 West 57th Street, 245-5000
Park Lane Hotel, 36 Central Park South, 371-4000
Petrossian, 182 West 58th Street, 245-2214
Plaza Hotel, The Oak Bar and Oyster Bar, Fifth Avenue at 59th Street, 759-3000
Rainbow Grill, 30 Rockefeller Plaza, 632-5100
Jimmy Ray's, 729 Eighth Avenue, 246-8562

Ritz Carlton Hotel, The Jockey Club, 112 Central Park South, 664-7700

St. Moritz Hotel, Cafe de la Paix, 50 Central Park South, 755-5800

Sam's Restaurant, 152 West 52nd Street, 582-8700

Sardi's, 234 West 44th Street, 221-8440

✓ **Shout,** 124 West 43rd Street, 869-2088

B. Smith's, 771 Eighth Avenue, 247-2222

Southern Funk Cafe, 330 West 42nd Street, 564-6560

Tastings, 144 West 55th Street, 757-1160

Terranova Cafe, 18 West 38th Street, 391-2123

Top of the Sixes, 666 Fifth Avenue, 757-6662

21 Club, 21 West 52nd Street, 582-7200

Un Deux Trois, 123 West 44th Street, 354-4148

Warwick Hotel, Warwick Bar, 65 West 54th Street, 247-2700

Westside Cafe, 131 West 57th Street, no phone number

34TH TO 59TH STREET
(West of Fifth Avenue)
East

John Barleycorn, 209 East 45th Street, 986-1988

Berkshire Place Hotel, Rendez-Vous, 21 East 52nd Street, 753-5970

Billy's, 949 First Avenue, 355-8920

Brew's, 156 East 34th Street, 889-3369

Charlie Brown's Ale & Chop House, 200 Park Avenue, 661-2520

Billy Budd, Shelburne–Murray Hill Hotel, 303 Lexington Avenue, 686-0110

Joe Burns, 903 First Avenue, 759-6696

Cafe Grand Central, 28 Vanderbilt Avenue, 883-0009

✓ **PJ Clarke's,** 915 Third Avenue, 759-1650

Doral Park Avenue Hotel, Lobby Lounge, 70 Park Avenue, 687-7050

Dustin's, 834 Second Avenue, 687-6360

41st Precinct, 24 East 41st Street, 679-3565

The Four Seasons, 99 East 52nd Street, 754-9494
Grand Hyatt Hotel, Sun Garden and Trumpet's, Park
  Avenue at Grand Central, 883-1234
Harglo's Cafe, 974 Second Avenue, 759-9820
Helmsley Palace Hotel, Gold Room, Harry's New York
  Bar, Hunt Room, and Madison Room, 455 Madison
  Avenue, 888-7000
Hotel Elysée, Monkey Bar, 60 East 45th Street, 753-1066
✓ **Juke Box NYC,** 304 East 39th Street, 685-1556
La Bibliothèque, 341 East 43rd Street, 661-5757
Marmalade Park, 222 East 39th Street, 687-7803
Michael's Pub, 211 East 55th Street, 758-2272
O'Lunney's, 915 Second Avenue, 751-5470
The Oyster Bar, Grand Central Terminal, 490-6650
Pancho & Lefty, 206 East 50th Street, 319-4700
Regent East, 204 East 58th Street, 355-9465
Roosevelt Hotel, Crawdaddy, 45 East 45th Street, 687-1860
Round's, 303 East 53rd Street, 593-0807
Runyon's, 932 Second Avenue, 759-7801
St. Regis Sheraton, St. Regis Grill, 2 East 55th Street,
  753-4500
Smith & Wollensky, 201 East 49th Street, 753-1530
Sparks, 210 East 46th Street, 687-4855
Top of the Tower, First Avenue and 49th Street,
  355-7300
United Nations Plaza Hotel, First Avenue and 44th
  Street, 355-3400
Waldorf-Astoria Hotel, Peacock Alley, 301 Park
  Avenue, 871-4895
Westfall, 251 East 50th Street, 644-9555

ABOVE 59TH STREET (East of Central Park)

Alo Alo, 1030 Third Avenue, 838-4343
The Beach Cafe, 1326 Second Avenue, 988-7299
Bemelmans (*see* Carlyle Hotel), 35 East 76th Street,
  744-1600

The Boathouse Cafe, Central Park (Fifth Avenue and 72nd Street entrance), 517-2233

Brandy's, 235 East 84th Street, 650-1944

Brighton Grill and Oyster Bar, 1313 Third Avenue, 988-6663

Camelback & Central, 1403 Second Avenue, 249-8380

Caramba!!!! 1576 Third Avenue, 876-8838

Carlyle Hotel, Bemelmans and Carlyle Cafe, 35 East 76th Street, 744-1600

Churchill's, 1277 Third Avenue, 650-1618

Ciao Bella, 1311 Third Avenue, 288-2555

Elaine's, 1703 Second Avenue, 534-8103

Etcetera, 1470 First Avenue, 382-0122

Finnegan's Wake, 1361 First Avenue, 737-3664

✓ **Flanagans,** 1215 First Avenue, 472-0300

Friday's, 1152 First Avenue, 832-8512

Gregory's, 1149 First Avenue, 371-2220

Hanratty's, 1754 Second Avenue, 289-3200

Hudson Bay Inn, 1454 Second Avenue, 861-5683

Intermezzo, 1748 Second Avenue, 427-3106

Juanita's, 1309 Third Avenue, 517-3800

Le Relais, 712 Madison Avenue, 751-5108

Martell's, 1469 Third Avenue, 861-6110

Maxwell's Plum, 1181 First Avenue, 628-2100

Jim McMullen's, 1341 Third Avenue, 861-4700

J. G. Melon, 1291 Third Avenue, 744-0585

Mortimer's, 1057 Lexington Avenue, 517-6400

Panama City, 1572 First Avenue, 288-0999

Rascals, 1286 First Avenue, 734-2862

Regency Hotel, Regency Hotel Lounge, 540 Park Avenue, 759-4100

Rusty's, 1271 Third Avenue, 861-4518

Safari Grill, 1115 Third Avenue, 371-9090

Sam's Cafe, 1406 Third Avenue, 988-5300

Sign of the Dove, 1110 Third Avenue, 861-8080

The Surf Club, 415 East 91st Street, 410-1360

✓ **Tuba City Truck Stop,** 1700 Second Avenue, 996-6200

Wilson's, 1441 First Avenue, 861-0320

59TH TO 72ND STREET
(West of Central Park)

All State Cafe, 250 West 72nd Street, 874-1883
Cafe des Artistes, 1 West 67th Street, 877-3500
Cafe Luxembourg, 200 West 70th Street, 873-7411
Columbus, 201 Columbus Avenue, 799-8090
Fountain Cafe, Lincoln Center, no phone number
Ginger Man, 51 West 64th Street, 724-7272
The Maestro Cafe, 58 West 65th Street, 787-5990
Mayflower Hotel, The Conservatory, 15 Central Park
    West, 581-0896
Palssons, 158 West 72nd Street, 362-2590
Ruppert's, 269 Columbus Avenue, 873-9400
√**The Saloon,** 1920 Broadway, 874-1500
Tavern on the Green, Central Park at 67th Street,
    873-3200

ABOVE 72ND STREET
(West of Central Park)

Bud's (Isabella's), 359 Columbus Avenue, 724-2100
Caramba!!! 2567 Broadway, 749-5055
Grapes, 522 Columbus Avenue, 362-3004
√ **Lucy's Restaurant,** 503 Columbus Avenue, 787-3009
Metropolis Restaurant, 444 Columbus Avenue, 769-4444
Museum Cafe, 366 Columbus Avenue, 799-0150
Silverbirds, 505 Columbus Avenue, 877-7777
The Terrace, 400 West 119th Street, 666-9490
West End Cafe, 2911 Broadway, 666-8750
The Works Bar, 428 Columbus Avenue, 799-7365

BARS BY RATING

THE <u>M</u>ETRIC
<u>M</u>ARTINI <u>M</u>EASUREMENT
<u>S</u>YSTEM: Mmms . . .

No martinis; not worth the trip. Better you should stay home with a bottle of Ripple and a good rerun.

Worth the visit; reasonable, fun bar. Drop in. A good drink-and-go.

Anything resembling a double is definitely worth a visit. Good buzz. *Go*.

A definite must-see; check out. If you haven't been here for drinks, don't admit it. Don't drive—*run*.

A drinking paradise. Milton move over. Beats everything else in life worth doing.

FOUR-MARTINI BARS

Algonquin Hotel Lounge
Helmsley Palace Hotel,
   Gold Room; Hunt
   Room; and Madison
   Room
Marriott Marquis Hotel,
   The View Bar
The Odeon
Plaza Hotel, The Oak Bar
Ritz Carlton Hotel, The
   Jockey Club
✓ Windows on the World

THREE-MARTINI BARS

Arthur's Tavern
Automatic Slims
The Bar
The Beach Cafe
Bellini
Cafe des Artistes
Cafe Luxembourg
Cafe Society
Carlyle Hotel, Bemel-
   mans; Carlyle Cafe
✓ PJ Clarke's
Curtain Up!
Delmonico's
Duplex
The Eagle's Nest
Elaine's
Five Oaks
The Four Seasons
Ginger Man
Harry's at Hanover
   Square
Heartbreak
Indochine
I Tre Merli Inc.

Juanita's
La Bibliothèque
Limelight
Lola
Marie's Crisis
Maxwell's Plum
Jim McMullen's
Michael's Pub
Mortimer's
Nell's
North River Bar
One Fifth
✓ One If by Land
Parker Meridien Hotel,
   Bar Montparnasse
Rainbow Grill
Raoul's
Regency Hotel, Regency
   Hotel Lounge
River Cafe
Round's
Rusty's
St. Regis Sheraton, St.
   Regis Grill

Sam's Cafe
✓ Shout
S.O.B.'s
Sofi
Southern Funk Cafe
Stringfellows
Tavern on the Green
Top of the Tower

✓ Tuba City Truck Stop
23rd Street Bar & Grill
Un Deux Trois
Union Square Cafe
J.S. VanDam
Waldorf-Astoria Hotel,
    Peacock Alley

TWO-MARTINI BARS

Joe Allen
All State Cafe
Art Cafe
The Ballroom
Bandito West
Bar Lui
Bayamo
Berkshire Place Hotel,
    Rendez-Vous
The Boathouse Cafe
Boy Bar
Bradley's Restaurant
Brandy's
Brighton Grill and Oyster
    Bar
Cafe Grand Central
Caramba!
Century Cafe
✓ Chevys
China Grill
Chumley's
Claire Restaurant
Columbus
The Cubbyhole
Don't Tell Mama

Doral Park Avenue Hotel
Dukie's
Empire Diner
Etcetera
Finnegan's Wake
Formerly Joe's
41st Precinct
Fountain Cafe
4D
Friday's
Gotham Bar and Grill
Grand Hyatt Hotel, Sun
    Garden
Gregory's
The Grove Club
Hanratty's
Harglo's Cafe
Harvey's Chelsea Restau-
    rant
Helmsley Palace Hotel,
    Harry's New York Bar
How's Bayou Cafe
Intermezzo
Jezebel
Juke Box NYC

Kingfisher
La Gamelle
The Landmark Tavern
Lavin's
Le Relais
The Lion's Head
Lucy's Restaurant
Dan Lynch Bar and Restaurant
The Maestro Cafe
Man Ray Bistro
Marmalade Park
Marriott Marquis Hotel, Broadway Lounge; JW's
Martell's
J. G. Melon
Metropolis Cafe
Mike's American Bar & Grill
The Milk Bar
Mumbles
Museum Cafe
Novotel, Novotel Wine Bistro
Old Town Bar & Restaurant
O'Neals
The Oyster Bar
Palio
Palladium
Palssons
Panama City
Petrossian
Plaza Hotel, Oyster Bar
Private Eyes Inc.
Quatorze

Rascals
Jimmy Ray's
Regent East
Rick's 181 Lounge
Roosevelt Hotel, Crawdaddy
Runyon's
St. Moritz Hotel, Cafe de la Paix
The Saloon
Sardi's
Savage
Sign of the Dove
Smith & Wollensky
B. Smith's
√ South Street Seaport
√ Sporting Club
Sunset Strip
The Surf Club
Tapis Rouge
Tastings
1018
Terranova Cafe
Tortilla Flats
Two Eleven Bar & Restaurant
Uncle Charlie's Downtown
Vazac's
Water Club
West End Cafe
√ The White Horse Tavern
Wine Bar
The Works Bar
The World

ONE-MARTINI BARS

Alo Alo
America
John Barleycorn
Barocco
Barrymore's
Between the Bread
Big Kahuna
Billy's
The Blue Mill Tavern
Brew's
Charlie Brown's Ale &
  Chop House
Bruxelles
Billy Budd
Bud's (Isabella's)
Joe Burns
Cafe 43
Cafe Madeleine
✓ Caliente Cab Company
Camelback & Central
Capsuoto Frères
Chapiteau Restaurant
Chez Ma Tante
Churchill's
Ciao Bella
✓ Covent Gardens
Jimmy Day's
Dustin's
✓ Ear Inn
Fanelli's Cafe
✓ Flanagans
Florent
Frank's
Grand Hyatt, Trumpet's
Grapes
Great Jones Cafe

Greene Street Cafe
Greensleeves
Hard Rock Cafe
✓ Holiday Cocktail Lounge
  & Restaurant
Hotel Elysée, Monkey Bar
Hudson Bay Inn
Il Palazzo
The Improvisation
Julius
King Tut's Wah Wah Hut
Mayflower Hotel, The
  Conservatory
✓ McSorley's Old Ale House
Metropolis Restaurant
Night Birds Restaurant &
  Bar
O'Lunney's
Pancho & Lefty
Pete's Tavern
Prince Street Bar & Res-
  taurant
Provence
Puffy's
Rectangles
Riverrun Cafe
Riviera Cafe
Ruppert's
Safari Grill
Sam's Restaurant
Shelter
Siberia
Silverbirds
Smoke Stacks Lightning
The Soho Kitchen and Bar
Sparks

The Terrace
Tunnel
21 Club
Twenty Twenty
United Nations Plaza
   Hotel Bar

Westfall
Westside Cafe
Wilson's
Woody's
Zig Zag

NO-MARTINI BARS

X Cadillac Bar
Chelsea Place
The New Deal
Park Lane Hotel

Top of the Sixes
Warwick Bar
X West 4th Street Saloon

BARS BY CATEGORY

BARS & BURGERS

Joe Allen
Billy's
Chumley's
PJ Clarke's
Fanelli's Cafe
Jimmy Day's
The Landmark Tavern
The Lion's Head
Museum Cafe
O'Lunney's

Pete's Tavern
Prince Street Bar & Restaurant
Jimmy Ray's
Rectangles
Ruppert's
Westfall
The White Horse Tavern
Woody's

BARS WITH OUTDOOR CAFES

Art Cafe
Bandito West
Bud's (Isabella's)
Caliente Cab Company
Capsuoto Frères
Chez Ma Tante
Curtain Up!
Jimmy Day's
Formerly Joe's
Grapes
How's Bayou Cafe
Le Relais

Metropolis Restaurant
Pete's Tavern
Rectangles
Riviera Cafe
St. Moritz Hotel, Cafe de la Paix
The Saloon
Silverbirds
West 4th Street Saloon
Westside Cafe
The White Horse Tavern

BARS FOR OUT-OF-TOWN GUESTS

Algonquin Hotel Lounge
The Boathouse Cafe
Fountain Cafe
The Four Seasons
Marriott Marquis Hotel
Plaza Hotel, The Oak
  Bar
Rainbow Grill
River Cafe

St. Moritz Hotel, Cafe de
  la Paix
Sparks
Tavern on the Green
The Terrace
Top of the Sixes
United Nations Plaza
  Hotel
Windows on the World

BARS WITH A VIEW

The Boathouse Cafe
La Bibliothèque
Marriott Marquis Hotel
Rainbow Grill
River Cafe

The Terrace
Top of the Sixes
Top of the Tower
Windows on the World

DANCE BARS

Boy Bar
Chevys
Dukie's
4D
Heartbreak
Juke Box NYC
Limelight
Nell's
North River Bar
Palladium

Savage
Shout
Siberia
S.O.B.'s
Stringfellows
The Surf Club
1018
Tunnel
The World

ENTERTAINMENT BARS

Arthur's Tavern
The Ballroom
Bradley's Restaurant
Carlyle Hotel
Chelsea Place
Greene Street Cafe
Hotel Elysée, Monkey Bar
The Improvisation
Dan Lynch Bar and Restaurant

Michael's Pub
Nell's
O'Lunney's
Palssons
Siberia
S.O.B.'s
Sporting Club
Terranova Cafe
West End Cafe

GAY BARS

The Bar
Boy Bar
Claire Restaurant
The Cubbyhole
Don't Tell Mama
The Eagle's Nest
The Grove Club

Julius
Marie's Crisis
Private Eyes Inc.
Regent East
Round's
Uncle Charlie's Downtown
The Works Bar

HOTEL BARS

Algonquin Hotel, Algonquin Hotel Lounge
Berkshire Place Hotel, Rendez-Vous
Carlyle Hotel, Bemelmans; Carlyle Cafe
Doral Park Avenue Hotel, Lobby Lounge
Grand Hyatt Hotel, Sun Garden; Trumpet's
Helmsley Palace Hotel, Gold Room; Harry's New York Bar; Hunt Room; and Madison Room
Hotel Elyseé, Monkey Bar
Marriott Marquis Hotel, Broadway Lounge;

JW's; The View Bar
Mayflower Hotel, The
  Conservatory
Novotel, Novotel Wine
  Bistro
Parker Meridien Hotel,
  Bar Montparnasse
Park Lane Hotel, Park
  Lane Bar
Plaza Hotel, The Oak
  Bar; Oyster Bar
Regency Hotel, Regency
  Hotel Lounge
Ritz Carlton Hotel, The
  Jockey Club
Roosevelt Hotel, Craw-
  daddy
St. Moritz Hotel, Cafe de
  la Paix
St. Regis Sheraton, St.
  Regis Grill
Shelburne-Murray Hill
  Hotel, Billy Budd
United Nations Plaza
  Hotel
Waldorf-Astoria, Peacock
  Alley
Warwick Hotel, Warwick
  Bar

NEIGHBORHOOD BARS

All State Cafe
Bandito West
Billy's
The Blue Mill Tavern
Brew's
Bruxelles
Chumley's
Churchill's
Covent Gardens
Dustin's
Ear Inn
Etcetera
Fanelli's Cafe
Finnegan's Wake
Flanagans
Friday's
Grapes
Great Jones Cafe
Greensleeves
Gregory's
Hanratty's
Harglo's Cafe
Harvey's Chelsea Restaurant
Holiday Cocktail Lounge
  & Restaurant
How's Bayou Cafe
Hudson Bay Inn
Jim McMullen's
Mike's American Bar & Grill
Night Birds Restaurant & Bar
Old Town Bar & Restaurant
Riverrun Cafe
Smoke Stacks Lightning
23rd Street Bar & Grill
Two Eleven
Vazac's

PIANO BARS

Carlyle Hotel, Bemelmans, Carlyle Cafe
Brandy's
Don't Tell Mama
Duplex
Five Oaks
Gregory's
Helmsley Palace Hotel,
Harry's New York Bar
Hotel Elyseé, Monkey Bar
Marie's Crisis
The New Deal
Regent East
St. Regis Sheraton, St. Regis Grill
Top of the Tower

RESTAURANT BARS

Alo Alo
America
John Barleycorn
Barocco
Bellini
Billy's
Bar Lui
The Beach Cafe
Between the Bread
Brighton Grill and Oyster Bar
Brew's
Charlie Brown's Ale & Chop House
Billy Budd Restaurant
Bud's (Isabella's)
Cafe des Artistes
Cafe 43
Cafe Grand Central
Cafe Luxembourg
Cafe Society
Caliente Cab Company
Camelback & Central
Capsuoto Frères
Century Cafe
Chapiteau Restaurant
Chez Ma Tante
China Grill
Churchill's
Ciao Bella
Claire Restaurant
Columbus
Covent Gardens
Roosevelt Hotel, Crawdaddy
Curtain Up!
Dustin's
Empire Diner
Etcetera
Finnegan's Wake
Flanagans
Florent
41st Precinct
The Four Seasons

Frank's
Friday's
Gotham Bar and Grill
Great Jones Cafe
Greensleeves
Hanratty's
Harglo's Cafe
Harvey's Chelsea Restaurant
Hudson Bay Inn
Il Palazzo
Indochine
Intermezzo
Jezebel
Jim McMullen's
J. G. Melon
Ritz Carlton, The Jockey Club
Juanita's
La Bibliothèque
La Gamelle
Lavin's
Le Relais
The Lion's Head
Lola
Lucy's Restaurant
The Maestro Cafe
Man Ray Bistro
Marmalade Park
Martell's
Maxwell's Plum
Metropolis Cafe
Metropolis Restaurant
Mike's American Bar & Grill
Mortimer's
Mumbles

Museum Cafe
The New Deal
Night Birds Restaurant & Bar
The Odeon
O'Neals
One Fifth
Oyster Bar at the Plaza
Palio
Panama City
Pancho & Lefty
Pete's Tavern
Petrossian
Provence
Quatorze
Raoul's
Rascals
Riverrun Cafe
Runyon's
Rusty's
The Saloon
Sam's Restaurant
Shelter
Sign of the Dove
Silverbirds
Sofi
Southern Funk Cafe
Smith & Wollensky
Sparks
Sunset Strip
Tapis Rouge
Tavern on the Green
The Terrace
Terranova Cafe
Tortilla Flats
Tuba City Truck Stop
21 Club

Twenty Twenty
23rd Street Bar & Grill
Two Eleven
Un Deux Trois
Union Square Cafe

J.S. VanDam
Water Club
Westfall
Westside Cafe
Wilson's

ROMANTIC BARS

The Boathouse Cafe
Cafe des Artistes
Gotham Bar and Grill
Lola
One If by Land
Petrossian
Rainbow Grill
River Cafe

Sign of the Dove
Sofi
Tapis Rouge
The Terrace
Top of the Tower
Water Club
Windows on the World

SPORTS BARS

Runyon's
Rusty's

Sporting Club

THEATER BARS

Algonquin Hotel Lounge
Joe Allen
Barrymore's
Bellini
Between the Bread
Cafe 43
Cafe Madeleine
Century Cafe
Curtain Up!
Jezebel

The Maestro Cafe
Mike's American Bar &
  Grill
Novotel Wine Bistro
Palio
Jimmy Ray's
The Saloon
Sam's Restaurant
Sardi's

TRENDY BARS

Alo Alo
America
Art Cafe
Automatic Slims
Bar Lui
Barocco
Bayamo
Big Kahuna
Brighton Grill and Oyster
  Bar
Cadillac Bar
Cafe Luxembourg
Cafe Society
Caramba
Chapiteau Restaurant
China Grill
Ciao Bella
Columbus
Dukie's
Empire Diner
Florent
Indochine
Juanita's
Kingfisher

King Tut's Wah Wah Hut
La Gamelle
Lola
Lucy's Restaurant
Man Ray Bistro
Metropolis Cafe
The Milk Bar
Mortimer's
Nell's
The Odeon
Private Eyes Inc.
Raoul's
Rick's 181 Lounge
Sam's Cafe
Savage
Sporting Club
Sunset Strip
1018
Tuba City Truck Stop
Twenty Twenty
Un Deux Trois
Union Square Cafe
J.S. VanDam

WINE BARS

I Tre Merli Inc.
Lavin's
Novotel Wine Bistro
Sofi

The Soho Kitchen and
  Bar
Tastings
Wine Bar

THE

BARS

ALGONQUIN HOTEL LOUNGE
59 West 44th Street (between Fifth and Sixth Avenues)
☎ 840-6800

A traditional watering hole for the literary set, the hotel lobby bar of the Algonquin is just about as special as you get in New York. Casual but formal, elegant but under-stated, the Algonquin has been something of a star on the New York bar scene for years. And when you visit, the reason is quite apparent. Occupying the majority of the lobby, the Algonquin Lounge offers an extremely comfortable living-room setting reminiscent of an English country house with dark wood paneling, humpbacked sofas, deep wing chairs, polished butler tables, fresh flowers, and a wonderful grandfather clock. Clusters of furniture are arranged for privacy and intimacy for the lounge's special crowd. You will not find a hot, stylish, or trendy crowd here, but rather an extremely interesting mixture of in-telligent, well-bred, and cultured patrons. Businessmen, theatergoers, tourists, and writers dress in everything from Shetlands to blazers and discuss Sartre, Nichols, Sinatra, and Saigon. Perfect for casual and elegant drinks before theater—or come back on a cold night with friends for a B&B. Equally exciting for die-hard New Yorkers and out-of-towners alike. Comfortable, inspirational, and, not un-like a fine wine, something to be savored.

JOE ALLEN
326 West 46th Street (between Eighth and Ninth Avenues)
☎ 581-6464

Another classic in the theater district commonly fre-quented by theater and film folk. Located on restaurant row, relatively small, crowded, and noisy, Joe Allen is a perfect place to meet for informal drinks before theater.

Joe Allen's chalkboard menu is served amidst red-checkered tablecloths. The bar, running the length of the restaurant, is equally busy and good-natured; catering to a mixed and eclectic crowd—wealthy matrons from Old Brookville mix with starving actors. Predominantly friends on their way to theater, the crowd is cliquish and stays mainly unto themselves. Drinks are moderately priced, the staff is young and courteous; all hold SAG/AFTRA union cards. The draw here is its frenetic theater energy—where producers, actors, and audience eat, drink, and mingle in anticipation of a night in the thea-ter. There's no people like show people . . .

ALL STATE CAFE
250 West 72nd Street (between Broadway and West End Avenue)
☎ 874-1883

West Side cozy, far enough away from Columbus Avenue and visiting throngs, the All State Cafe's downstairs pub surely qualifies as a neighborhood bar. Homey, pretension-free, and comfortable, All State is modeled after the small-town cafes found in the Main Streets of Southwest America. And apparently the formula of plain wooden furniture, dim lighting, excellent chili, and tasty burgers works. There is something to be said for a neighborhood haunt where one can feel comfortable and at ease knowing few tourists or "burb people" are likely to invade. The crowd here lives and breathes West Side air. It's rare here to find any snobbery or elitism polluting the atmosphere. During the day, perfect to wander in and feel comfortable alone sipping beer. At night, consider yourself lucky to get a seat. Bring your own saddle.

ALO ALO
1030 Third Avenue (at 61st Street)
☎ 838-4343

Not unlike the Italian railway system—slow, dirty, and undependable, this Upper East Side watering hole for the young, the restless, and the Italian still manages to pack them in. Centrally located on prime Third Avenue Bloomingdale's turf, the bar at Alo Alo must be doing something right. Attractive yuppies and assorted East Side trendies pack the bar—particularly during cocktail hour. It is slick, sophisticated, and lit like a Hollywood set; lots of the East Side folk stay on and indulge in a pasta pig-out. I guess what they don't know, doesn't hurt: At all extremes and at all expenses, don't bother staying on for dinner. Let's just say that you can count on your train to arrive on schedule in Naples more than you can count on a dependable dinner in this establishment. Need I say more? For drinks—fun for a splash; for dinner—bye-bye to Alo Alo.

AMERICA
9 East 18th Street (between Fifth Avenue and Broadway)
☎ 505-2110

If the restaurant scene has been moving in the direction of serving up theatrics these days, then America certainly stands center stage. Absolutely immense, cavernous, crowded, and yuppie to the hilt, America places as much emphasis on architecture as on food. Eating in this space must add a most distinctive flavor to your meal. And if America doesn't continue to make it as a restaurant, you can't help but think that all they would have to do is close the doors for a couple of hours to reopen as a discotheque. Imagine having dinner in a brightly lit disco club and you have the feel of America. Loud buzz, frenetic pace, and tables situated out on what would be the dance floor. Even the neon fixtures work. Just add a strobe light. When you enter the room, your eye is immediately drawn to the rear wall where the bar is elevated and runs the wide expanse of the restaurant. Stand there and feel as if you are at a bar waiting for a good dance song to come on. You find a large open area with lots of space to stand comfortably. Perhaps America is trying to redefine singles bars of the eighties—"Let's not ostracize the singles bar scene but incorporate it into our living room and make it part of our very hip and crowded trendy restaurant." But America just doesn't cut it anymore. Overexposure coupled with newer and trendier bars in the neighborhood has taken away its initial draw. A third-rate crowd filled with students and Staten Island folk remains. In other words, a "let's go to the city and be cool" crowd. As a space, something to be experienced. As a bar, a has-been. If this is America the beautiful, then God shed his waste on thee.

ART CAFE
151 Second Avenue (between 9th and 10th Streets)
☎ 598-0366

If you take an evening stroll down Second Avenue below 14th Street, you can't help but feel how the East Village has become the hottest part of town. Sidewalks filled with tourists, drug dealers, hippies, yuppies, neighborhood performance artists, con artists, and derelicts sizzle with energy. When you want to cool out but want to remain in the swing of things, check out this neighborhood spot with a decor as lively as its clientele. Its loud interior, fueled by a never-ending supply of East Village new-wave cassettes, seems to include every playful decoration known to man. The colorful tropical decor is dominated by synthetic palm trees artistically wrapped around water pipes.

Vibrant orange, pink, and green walls are adorned with pictures of the Statue of Liberty, Washington Square Arch, and a bold French poster. Mirrors, Christmas lights, hanging colored tinsel, kitsch latticework, plastic fruit, and psychedelic spray painting may prove to be a sensory overload. But its young staff parallels its surroundings by shouting orders back and forth to one another while still finding the time to meet and greet their regulars. Many locals come with friends, and those who know the staff tend to drink at the informal eleven-seat bar or at its adjacent tables decorated with whimsical martini graphics. Weather permitting, a large streetside cafe with roomy tables attracts an interesting preppie-to-punk crowd drinking, dining, and desserting. Come and soak up local color from Art Cafe's vibrant palette. If art is defined by color and form, then Art Cafe successfully offers both.

ARTHUR'S TAVERN

57 Grove Street (between Seventh Avenue and Bleecker Street)

☎ 675-6879

Wedged in between the "Broadway Belters" on Grove Street is a real find, Arthur's Tavern. Old, dark, seedy, and small, Arthur's Tavern offers hot and steamy, down-and-dirty jazz. In other words, don't come here expecting to hear "How Do You Solve a Problem like Maria" in four-part harmony. It's a great place to come to hear a jazz combo (piano, bass, drums) at very affordable prices. A mixed drink runs $3, but you can have no problem making it last through a set or two. The crowd is very mixed; predominantly straight, some yuppie, some sleazy, young and old, uptown and downtown, and gets cooking *late*. It's a wonderful dive to stop in at two A.M., have a Scotch on the rocks, hold hands with a date, wear dark sunglasses, and get your libido going. The place looks as if it is decorated for Christmas and St. Patrick's Day—

even during the summer. It's as if they were looking for a holiday that lasts all year as an excuse to celebrate continually. At Arthur's Tavern, you *can* deck the halls, for it is always a holiday.

AUTOMATIC SLIMS
733 Washington Street (at Bank Street)
☎ 645-8660

One of the hottest new bars to open its doors in the Far West Village is, quite simply, a bar long overdue. Few can dispute the West Village's need for a hot, happening, interesting, exciting straight bar. I am pleased to report that the new addition of Automatic Slims is exactly on target. Housed in the former corner Villa Eda restaurant on Bank Street, Automatic Slims doesn't look like much from the outside; and its appropriately small, clean, uncluttered white brick interior punctuated by rock 'n' roll, James Brown, and Brigitte Bardot posters certainly can't take credit for the success. The attraction and excitement at this new Bank Street bistro is in the crowd. A strikingly attractive thirty-ish crowd, with lots of Tribeca arty models and actors, combines good preppie looks with what appears to be interesting character. Although the bar is SRO crowded, you can call ahead and reserve a table for a light dinner. Lots of friends come with friends, but a lively, noisy, upbeat atmosphere makes it easy to make some new friends—even if it's just for the evening. Chances are slim that you won't automatically enjoy yourself at this new and refreshing neighborhood hot spot.

THE BALLROOM

253 West 28th Street (between Seventh and Eighth Avenues)

☎ 244-3005

An elegant and hip Chelsea bar, restaurant, and cabaret all rolled into one. A clean, bright, inviting restaurant with large potted palm trees, strolling violinists, and waiters hustling and bustling in starched black-and-white uniforms make this setting perfect for a celebration. Raised up about three steps, in the back of the restaurant, is the very crowded bar. Interestingly, one does not go to the bar at The Ballroom for drinks, as much as one goes to sample all of the wonderful food available at the bar. Perhaps one of the most lavish and savory tapas buffets of its kind, the bar offers an amazing assortment of hors d'oeuvres prepared by The Ballroom's kitchen, ranging from tasty chicken dishes to pig's knuckles. Each platter is labeled and priced accordingly. Expect a $15 tab for two drinks and one of the hors d'oeuvres. The crowd is well-heeled and tends to be older yet very mixed—East Side divorcées in mink coats, West Side men, lots of expense accounts, blazers, ties, and most with friends. Some make a meal and an evening out of the appetizers and drinks, while others are en route into yet another part of The Ballroom—the nightclub. The nightclub at The Ballroom presents entertainment ranging from Wayland Flowers to Karen Akers to Martha Raye. A high-techy gray and black tiered mirrored room is sophisticated and stylish, yet intimate. An average show will charge a $15 cover with a two-drink minimum, and reservations are required. Although pricey, and a bit on the dressy side, The Ballroom's draw is variety. In its appeal to all—the gourmets, the drinkers, and the clubbers—it certainly keeps its bases loaded. And in all likelihood, you will not strike out here.

BANDITO WEST

33 Greenwich Avenue (between West Tenth and Charles Streets)

☎ 807-0120

It's hard to find a better West Village spot to enjoy frosty margaritas on a hot summer night than this Greenwich Avenue hacienda. Though it's hard to believe, outdoor cafes specializing in Mexican warfare are not as easy to come by in New York as one would imagine. This one is really quite a joy. By definition, Greenwich Avenue takes you off the beaten path of mainstream Village carbon monoxide fumes and allows for more mellow street cruising. A lively outdoor patio with bright red chairs and matching umbrellas complement the playful black, white, and pop-art interior. The crowd parked here tends to be predominantly neighborhood, folks dressed in Bermuda shorts and Converse high-tops. The atmosphere is extremely laid-back, completely unrushed; most come with friends and enjoy each other's company. Tasty margaritas work their magic and serve as an easy lubricant for intimate conversation. Grab a corner table and dissect a finished love affair. Order another round and start a new one.

THE BAR

Second Avenue and 4th Street

☎ no phone number

You cannot possibly find a more East Village gay bar than The Bar. On the corner of 4th Street and Second Avenue, diagonally across from the Saint, this dark, sleazy, and grungy corner bar has certainly held its corner in a very busy marketplace. The green tattered and stained awning welcoming its patrons outside proves to be a good indication of what to expect. Sleazy and surprisingly comfortable, The Bar attracts a late-night East Village neighborhood crowd. The place is filled with young, hardworking (or hardly working) artists-to-be, political and literary types, waiters, dancers, muffin-bakers, apartment-cleaners, and even attractive boys to boot. For pickups and the "let's exchange numbers" scene, the witching hour doesn't start until midnight. By one A.M. the joint is jumping, with enough hormones in the air to start a beard growing on Renee Richards. As gay bars go, The Bar keeps "attitude" down to a minimum and makes it relatively easy to cross the barrier to meet your neighbors without having all the heavy sexual overtones. Dress is strictly Second Avenue Levi; an old pair of black paratrooper boots preferred. If the music on the jukebox doesn't take up your time (and change), you can always shoot pool with one of the neighborhood dykes. And when you just get too tired of checking everyone else out, check out your cue ball.

JOHN BARLEYCORN
209 East 45th Street (between Second and Third Avenues)
☎ 986-1988

U.S. and Irish flags fly in front of the well-lit green and white boxy building front that's housed this bar for over twenty years. As you enter, a ragged, hand-lettered sign says PROPER ATTIRE REQUIRED, but the dress ranges from three-piece suits to fairly casual. Smoke hangs heavy in this dimly lit room with brick and rough wood walls. A red banquette winds its way around the room and there are numerous tables available just for drinks. The bar itself is roomy and has a false roof that's as covered with business cards as the room is with businessmen and -women. There's live music nightly after nine P.M., except on Sunday when the bar is closed. The jukebox is filled with tunes like "Highland Paddy," "Galway Bay," "Days in Old Donegal," and of course, "When Irish Eyes Are Smiling."

BAR LUI

625 Broadway (between Bleecker and Houston Streets)
☎ 473-8787

The new hot strip in town, Lobro, an acronym for Lower Broadway, has given Columbus Avenue a sure run for its money. With its transplanted California record company, Tower Records, rolling down one of the first red carpets in the neighborhood, trendy retailers, clothing boutiques, condos, and Korean markets were quick to follow suit. Lobro is rapidly becoming highbrow. Amidst the trendy eateries that have nestled into the neighborhood is a large, loud, pretty, and moderately priced Italian restaurant, Bar Lui. A definite trendy addition to the neighborhood, Lui boasts a large open space, white walls, blue and pink neon lighting, deco lines, and punk haircuts. The restaurant is large, the tables are small, the noise level is high, and the attractive crowd is a mixture of Village, Soho, and uptown. The bar area, situated at the very front of the restaurant, is busy. It seems that as many folks are coming to Bar Lui for the bar as for the food. Drinks are reasonably priced; the staff is young, courteous, and interesting to watch. The crowd is on the young side, with lots of leather jackets, trendy black-and-white outfits, and some NYU'ers thrown in. If you can manage to shout over the restaurant din, it's a good place to go with friends and perhaps meet some new ones. At the moment, Lui is very New York—but hurry on down, for today's drinking hot spot might very well be tomorrow's condominium.

BAROCCO
301 Church Street (near Canal Street)
☎ 431-1445

It's hard to say what will strike you first when you enter
this Tribeca trattoria—its clean, white, deco-inspired space,
or its ear-shattering decibel level. One thing you can't help
but notice is how the downtown Tribeca crowd has found
a pasta palace of their very own. The simple bar at Barocco
doesn't look particularly substantial—a simple frameless
mirror and a few Memphis-inspired black chairs serve as
a holding ground for diners awaiting tables. But at around
ten P.M., a strikingly slick clientele, dressed in an array
from black leather to blue jeans, seemingly comes out of
the woodwork. By eleven P.M., conversations at the bar,
looking like something out of a Marx Brothers movie, are
consistently punctuated with "What did you say?" But if
you're in the mood for loud, frenetic, downtown drinks
with patrons packed together like sardines, *ciao*.

BARRYMORE'S
267 West 45th Street (between Broadway and Eighth Avenue)
☎ 541-4500

This Broadway baby, located in the heart of the theater
district, offers a convenient, comfortable, and simple bar.
The long wooden bar runs the length of the front room
and one can feel equally at ease sitting down with a book
in tow or with a friend. Decor is Broadway standard—
theater posters, playbills, and memorabilia line the walls.
The crowd tends to be an older down-to-earth bunch, many
of whom work or have worked in the business. Popular
with actors, stage folk, technicians, and other theater aspirants; it would make sense that business peaks before
and after performance time. This joint has been around

for ages, and, from the looks of it, will continue to settle in to its "long-run" engagement.

BAYAMO

705 Broadway (near Washington Place)

☎ 475-5151

You find a large paper palm tree framing the floor-to-ceiling window in this two-leveled lower Broadway spectacle. Bayamo's striking wall-to-wall mural, undulating balcony, and dramatic pink tubular lighting are interesting and exciting enough reasons to check out this Chinese-Cuban addition to Lobro. Imagine if all the Eighth Avenue greasy Chinese-Cuban places closed their kitchens, pooled their money, and opened a yuppie restaurant to establish a place in the trendy world of upscale restaurants. Design it between Tower Records and Unique Clothing, and the trend becomes quite a success. A large twenty-five-seat bar is absolutely jam-packed weekends and attracts a lively midweek crowd as well. The crowd tends to be Lobro locals and Tower Records dropouts. A lot of friends come with friends and loners can make themselves at home during the day. The interior is quite simply a knockout; exposed gray columns, live palm trees, deco lighting fixtures, and a large and brilliantly colored Gauguin-like mural is an absolute scene-stealer. This is certainly restaurant theatrics at its finest. Dress for the part. Fun, lively, and at the moment, trendy.

THE BEACH CAFE
1326 Second Avenue (at 70th Street)
☎ **988-7299**

Can't make it to Cape Cod? If you're citybound, the Beach Cafe should buoy your spirits. The walls are covered with refreshing views of the seashore that vary from bold, semi-abstract oil paintings, to pastel landscapes, to black-and-white photographs. The artwork is for sale with prices ranging from $200 to $1,000. Dinner will cost you much less, though, and you can choose between salads, burgers, sixteen kinds of pasta or a variety of entrees. Pink globe lights with rattan shades lend the room a cheery warmth and soften the tile floors, brick walls, and pressed tin ceiling. The turn-of-the-century saloon-style mahogany bar is also a work of art; it seats about fifteen people. There's a large porch with an intimate atmosphere that wraps around the main room and offers sidewalk scenery. The crowd is mostly thirty and up and their idea of the beach is likely to be Palm Beach or the Riviera. No beach bums, please, as proper attire is required. J&B Scotch has a courtesy car, a Rolls Royce, that frequently stops by. If you see it out front, speak to the maître d'; they'll be more than happy to give you a lift home.

BELLINI
777 Seventh Avenue (at 51st Street)
☎ **265-7770**

Forget the family feud caused by closing Harry Cipriani in the Sherry Netherland and stenciling in the new name "Tino Fontana" on the door between lunch and dinner. Forget front-page coverage by *The New York Times* of this takeover by Trusthouse Forte. Forget Harry Cipriani's well-publicized letter to *New York Times* restaurant reviewer

Bryan Miller citing inaccuracies in his review of Harry Cipriani's and his request that Miller not review his newest restaurant, Bellini. Forget it all because Harry Cipriani's Bellini is a true delight and quite simply an extraordinary spot for sophisticated drinks. Small, intimate, and chic, Bellini is modeled after the legendary Harry's Bar in Venice, which was opened in 1931 on the Calle Vallaresso, a few steps from the Grand Canal. Throughout the thirties, Harry's Bar was frequented by everyone from Charlie Chaplin and Noel Coward to Georges Braque and the Duke and Duchess of Windsor. While retaining a similar aura of idiosyncrasy and glamor, Bellini continues to draw all the A players. Gstaad, St. Moritz, the moneyed and titled set dine in this mecca for the ultrarich and the pampered. Recreating Harry's original atmosphere, Bellini is brightly lit with low ceilings, pale peach fabrics, art deco fixtures, and short, small cocktail tables crowded together in the way tables tend to be in bars. The ladies who lunch here, draped in Chanel, are deposited safely from waiting limousines. Most pass through the tiny jewel of a bar directly to waiting tables. Stocked with a healthy share of present-day Hemingways, Gertrude Steins, Mames and Vera Charleses, Bellini is perfect for star Broadway drinking. This is one ticket that won't disappoint. Here for a long run.

BERKSHIRE PLACE HOTEL
21 East 52nd Street (at Madison Avenue)
☎ 753-5970

RENDEZ-VOUS One of the most popular after-work spots for the over-thirty executive world, the Rendez-Vous manages to draw a crowd night after night. This large bar and restaurant, located right off the lobby of an Omni-owned hotel, has been cleverly designed with sections of tables placed and divided by brass railings and raised partitions creating small and separate islands. The place itself is pretty—Victorian-style lighting fixtures augment the soft earthy decor. Without this clever floor plan, the room would be a massive sea of bodies. There are lots of executives and out-of-towners, business meetings and office socializing, with everyone dressed in suits and dresses. Lots of white button-down shirts and good attaché cases can be seen leaving the checkroom. The bar itself begins to fill up at five P.M. and continues to pack in a crowd right until eight P.M. Convenient for advertising and public-relations executives, the Rendez-Vous appears to have lots of eligible men (you can't help but notice how the men outnumber the women here) leaving their offices for more pleasant surroundings and perhaps an interesting diversion. Free hors d'oeuvres and crudités make it easy to satisfy end-of-the-day hunger pangs.

BETWEEN THE BREAD

145 West 55th Street (between Sixth and Seventh Avenues)

☎ 581-1189

Pink, peach, and pretty, midtown comfortable and quiet, Between the Bread offers the triple-header of bar, restaurant, and bakery. Tucked away in the far corner of the restaurant and offering a good view of 55th Street, the sleek bar at Between the Bread comfortably seats eight, and offers additional cocktail table seating. Convenient to Carnegie Hall and to City Center, Between the Bread seems to be an insider's place to rendezvous. As a result, if you are looking for a quiet, comfortable, and relaxed spot to meet and be alone and quiet with a friend, this is well worth a try. Otherwise, choose one of the livelier places just moments away in this very busy part of town.

BIG KAHUNA

622 Broadway (between Bleecker and Houston Streets)

☎ 460-9633

It's hard to find a better means of escape from the summer's heat than by wading down to this lower Broadway club. Wear the latest from Laguna, rub a little zinc oxide on the nose, don your Vuarnets, and by all means don't leave home without your surfboard. Ordering a Scotch and water at the bar is about as close to water as this New York surfer crowd gets. Thriving on the lively decor, the crowd is encouraged to act as if they are on vacation. The floor is carpeted with sand, the walls have a shacklike finish, and one wall boasts a sixty-foot turquoise wave threatening to break on the crowd—complete with a shark's jaws clenching a surfer's legs. And what would vacation fun be without hamburgers, hot dogs, and Frisbees. Add bikini-clad women serving drinks, retro music, and video screens, and temperatures are bound to rise. Expect not only to have to fight a crowd to get in, but a $5 cover on Wednesday, Thursday, and after eight P.M. Fridays and Saturdays. Try checking out the scene after work—a comfortable Noho neighborhood crowd mixes with Soho'ers, Wall Streeters heading home, and NYU residents. When it's hazy, hot, and humid—try to be cooler at Kahuna. Everybody else does.

BILLY'S

949 First Avenue (near 52nd Street)

☎ 355-8920

If you want to capture the feel of a real old-fashioned saloon in midtown's far East Side, this might be a good choice. Established in 1870, Billy's is predominantly a steak house and is accordingly decorated with requisite red checkered tablecloths, tiled floor, sawdust, and hand-some, weathered bar. Patronized by an older, well-heeled East Side crowd, the bar at Billy's is frequented mostly by customers awaiting tables. I would not let that stop you—particularly on a quiet snowy afternoon. The light filtering in through large glass windows lends itself to a restful sort of dreaminess. Bring a good friend or a warm novel. But, don't leave home without them.

THE BLUE MILL TAVERN
50 Commerce Street (off Bedford Street)
☎ 243-7114

Another former speakeasy tucked away next to the pic-turesque Cherry Lane Theater since 1926, the Blue Mill offers a rustic neighborhood tavern where one can relax, drink, eat, and be merry. Old fixtures, dark brown-stained booths, windmill murals, and warm lighting add to its neighborhood charm. Beware of a midnight closing—go early to enjoy the warmth and quiet. So quiet, you might even think you are out of New York. Off the beaten path, perfect for an out-of-the-way intimate rendezvous.

THE BOATHOUSE CAFE
Central Park (Fifth Avenue and 72nd-Street entrance)
☎ 517-2233

Central Park is undeniably one of the best gifts Manhattan has ever given itself. Smack in the middle of the "Concrete Jungle," this parcel of beauty brings joy to the thousands who visit each week. Like icing on a homemade cake, a large lake adds to the bucolic romance of its rolling lawns. The Boathouse Cafe, a brick colonial-style boathouse overlooking the lake, was built in 1954 and refurbished last year. It offers a wonderful view for outdoor drinks when the desire strikes to get away from Manhattan asphalt. Just a short hike away from Fifth Avenue and like a postcard from a European holiday, its large outdoor plank deck is divided into two sections. On one side, a full service restaurant offers dining under umbrella-capped tables. Immediately adjacent to the restaurant, smaller cocktail tables are set up exclusively for drinks. Unfortunately, the bar's overall presentation pales in comparison to the view. However, views of Central Park's skyline reflecting off the water far outweigh the plastic-cup and paper-napkin service. It's too bad, though—this spot has the potential to be an upscale elegant treat. At any rate, plan a sunset visit and remain long enough to watch the sky light up. As breathtaking as the planetarium can be, catch a clear night in the middle of Manhattan when the moon and stars are shining bright overhead and you realize there's no place like home.

BOY BAR

15 St. Mark's Place (between Second and Third Avenues)

☎ **674-9219**

Boy Bar lives up to its name. This is strictly a bar for boys. Alabaster-skinned boys who never seem to see the light of day, Boy George caps, and Pee Wee Herman boy clones pack this St. Mark's classic. Girls, however, waitress huge paper cups of beer to the thirsty crowd, particularly after sweating away time on the dance floor downstairs. The place itself isn't much to look at—East Village tackiness with linoleum floors and paint peeling from the walls. For a minimum cover ($5 before midnight, $8 thereafter), boys pour in from all directions until well after midnight to booze and boogie. Around for some time now, and not unlike an episode out of *Upstairs, Downstairs,* Boy Bar has changed its layout periodically and, from the looks of it, has settled on a large room for cruising, video, and live performances on the main floor, and a dance floor discreetly tucked away downstairs for hot and sweaty dancing. The bar upstairs is large and J-shaped and provides the focal point of the room. Video monitors mounted on the walls placate an eighties "let's have something to focus on" sensibility and can be seen from cabaret tables and chairs which are set up for the live show, which generally airs after midnight. As late as 1:30 A.M., the cordon leading to the steep stairway down is finally parted, and within a matter of minutes, the lower room fills up and the dance floor is packed. The downstairs disco palace reads tribal—small black bar, black walls, black ceiling, wood floor, a home-painted mural, simple overhead lamps, and huge floor-to-ceiling speakers that pump sexy music to the eager crowd. No fancy special effects, just loud music and a place to dance. It's two A.M. and the boys shift right into high gear without any warm-up. Crew cuts, young lean torsos, and high energy fill the room. Friends dance with friends and release energy. The room on the main floor has virtually emptied out; a few linger over video reruns. But it's clear, the action remains downstairs until closing. If you come expecting boy attitude, catch a good nap, and leave your healthy tan outside, then Boy Bar still offers a jolt of energy in an endangered small-club atmosphere.

BRADLEY'S RESTAURANT
70 University Place (between 10th and 11th Streets)
☎ 228-6440, 473-9700

A downtown Central Greenwich Village jazz club with a peculiarly serious uptown flavor. Long and narrow, paneled and brightly lit, Bradley's is a great spot to sip a gin and tonic and settle back to hear some jazz. Paintings lining the walls echo a sense of bohemia. With no cover charge and a comfortable long bar, you can easily combine an evening of drinking and enjoying some live music at a surprisingly affordable price. The music, usually a bass and piano, is consistently good, and takes center stage. If you go with a group of friends, get there before ten P.M., grab a table, and endure the $5 minimum. However, if you want to sit and talk with your friends make sure to arrive before the set begins. Because once the music starts, the voices surely stop, and everyone concentrates on the music. Conversation is rare here during musical sets, and often is greeted with, to say the least, unfriendly stares. Lots of "serious" jazz folk here. The bar itself does get a good mixture of people—couples, friends, and singles—from pipe-smoking intellectuals in Wallabees to Cheryl Tiegs types. The "universal language" sure manages to draw this eclectic mix. Dress casual but calculated and you'll fit right in in this somewhat schizo uptown-downtown haunt.

BRANDY'S

235 East 84th Street (between Second and Third Avenues)

☎ 650-1944

The black upright piano stands alone, its naked underbelly exposed to the pub, a goldfish bowl on top to receive donations. Come early when the music starts and brood a little . . . light a cigarette, gaze dreamily out the somewhat grimy window, and lose yourself in the lilting melodies of yesteryear. As the crowd picks up it becomes gayer, both in body and soul. Favorite songs are requested and pretty soon you find yourself singing along to songs you didn't even know you knew. Black pews encircle the main room, fronted by tiny cocktail tables right on top of each other. The brick walls are decorated with French cabaret posters and the whole place feels like a time warp. Although the crowd is mostly gay, a straight person should feel right at home here. Stay a while. Have a brandy. Music nightly from 9:30.

BREW'S

156 East 34th Street (between Third and Lexington Avenues)

☎ **889-3369**

For over fifty years this family-owned restaurant has been serving customers at this location. Although many of these loyal patrons are now over forty, the jukebox is aimed at the youth of the eighties, with groups like Fine Young Cannibals, Depeche Mode, and REM. A stuffed boar's head is mounted behind the bar; old black-and-white photographs, maps, and odd magazine pages hang on the brick walls. The amber light is hazy in the dark and narrow bar area, where many a Scotch and soda is served to the faithful after their long day's work.

BRIGHTON GRILL AND OYSTER BAR

1313 Third Avenue (between 75th and 76th Streets)

☎ **988-6663**

Thanks to careful planning and design, this rather small space feels clean, light, spacious and airy, even when crowded. Blue neon signs hang in both picture windows, with white Levolors and window boxes of delicate flowers in full bloom. The brick walls are painted white and you can almost see the ceiling fans twirl in the shiny parquet floor. A black-and-white checked motif is used sparingly and to good effect in the tiles of the bar and back wall. The bar is primarily white tile with a long expanse of mirrors broken by twisted wooden columns. Full meals are available and encouraged at the bar, and there's a raw buffet display at the front of the bar to rival the most chichi of sushi bars. The elegant floral arrangements include fresh fruits and vegetables and constitute works of art in themselves. Brighton does a big brunch business, but is not unmercifully crowded with the after-work crunch. The clientele is thirty and over, but more hip than in other area hot spots. Truly a breath of fresh air in a stuffy neighborhood.

CHARLIE BROWN'S ALE & CHOP HOUSE
200 Park Avenue (Pan Am Building; at 43rd Street)
☎ 661-2520

Located in the Pan Am Building right off Grand Central Terminal, Charlie Brown's is your typical old-fashioned Irish commuter bar. Lots of men, lots of beer, lots of smoke, and closed on weekends. Absolutely jam-packed during the week between the hours of five P.M. and seven P.M., Charlie Brown's caters to an older commuter clientele who seemingly come back day after day, month after month, year after year. And in honor of its twenty-year patrons, the management has mounted commemorative plaques on the bar as Christmas presents. The large square-shaped bar stands front and center in this nondescript room (which could easily pass for a suburban mall restaurant), and offers plenty of space for standing and enjoying cheese, crackers, and free hors d'oeuvres set out by old-fashioned bartenders. The crowd seems to be predominantly middle management, secretaries, and office managers on their way home to Yonkers. A domestic beer runs $2.75. It's too bad that Charlie Brown's prime location, large space, and free munchies don't draw a more interesting clientele.

BRUXELLES
118 Greenwich Avenue (at 13th Street)
☎ 206-1830

This West Village restaurant offers an intimate, quiet, and warm European-style bistro with lace curtains, brick walls, and shiny copper bar where one can feel comfortable stopping in with a couple of friends for drinks and laughs; with a lover for an intimate nightcap; or even alone to have a light supper served graciously at the bar and not feel conspicuous. This is what Bruxelles offers—comfort, relaxation, and the chance for you to make the kind of experience you desire. There are ten bar stools with room for another ten at five cocktail tables. A chalkboard lists eight different kinds of beers to choose from (ranging from $3.50 to $5), seven different types of champagne, and white wines served by the glass. Taped music plays quietly in the background—and the bartender is open to your requests. Dress strictly for comfort—this is not the place for trendiness. Unfortunately, this is a fireplace bar *without* a fireplace. It shouts out for one. What a perfect place to stop in for a B&B on a cold winter's night with a date after taking in a flick at the Greenwich.

BILLY BUDD
303 Lexington Avenue (Shelburne–Murray Hill Hotel; between 37th and 38th Streets)
☎ 686-0110

Once inside the stark marble foyer of the hotel, take a sharp right and you'll find yourself inside an intimate pub. The dim square room has a small semicircular bar with a nook above it holding mugs and seldom-read books. The room feels rustic with its wooden floor, ceiling fans, amber lighting, and candles on the brass-top tables that line the brick and wood-paneled back wall. They have Tennent, Whitbread, and other ales and beers on tap, and the bartender gives a disgusted look if someone should dare to order a nonalcoholic beverage. Ironically, under banners for Scotland, Ireland, England, and Wales, American men in three-piece suits drink martinis and discuss business in regional dialects that span this country.

BUD'S (now called Isabella's)
359 Columbus Avenue (at 77th Street)
☎ 724-2100

Expense-account diners grace this palm-tree pretty restaurant, owned by the folks who brought you East Side's Jam's. In the foyer of the restaurant, a small but attractive bar with six Parisian-style bar stools is used predominantly by the crowd awaiting a table for dinner. But the bar at Bud's is also perfect for a romantic nightcap on the way home from a night out on the town. Although Columbus Avenue offers a lot of outdoor cafes in which to do your drinking and sidewalk cruising, Bud's offers one of the prettiest and probably most elegant options: there's something to be said for crisp white linen tablecloths and sparkling crystal when you're eating outdoors. It's particularly glorious at sunset. Use your imagination, sit back, sip champagne, and pretend to be in Cannes on a sunny day in April. For that alone, it may very well be worth the visit.

JOE BURNS
903 First Avenue (at 51st Street)
☎ 759-6696

This First Avenue combination restaurant and art gallery has a real promising look and feel. An unobstructed glass facade highlighted by a neon EAT AT JOE's sign, a whimsical black-and-white tiled floor, red and black vinyl chairs, and a neon wall clock add a kind of unexpected funkiness to this part of town. Credit must go to owner and artist Joe Burns who uses his space not only as a restaurant, but also as a spot to exhibit his own artwork. Patrons come to Joe Burns predominantly for the restaurant, particularly on

Sunday mornings, to indulge in great French toast and hear live chamber music. Paper tablecloths and crayons add fun to the visit. The bar itself draws a late-night crowd, particularly on the weekend. Dress East Side fun, preferably something in black and white, and you will blend right in with the local clientele.

CADILLAC BAR
15 West 21st Street (between Fifth and Sixth Avenues)
☎ **645-7220**

Several years back the trend in fashionable dining included supplying paper tablecloths and crayons for patrons with a proclivity for doodling. Now, years later, as evidenced at Cadillac Bar, the concept has expanded to scribbling on walls, floors, ceilings, doors, and any other imaginable surface. Indeed, if the latest craze in restaurant design includes graffiti, then Cadillac Bar is a trailblazer. The latest addition to the flash and trash market in the West 20s, Cadillac Bar is sure packing the crowd in; it has lines snaking out the door. Running a full city block long, Cadillac Bar's space seems to be never-ending—with its high ceilings, poor acoustics, and hundreds of bodies in search of hundreds of other bodies. The place just seems to go on forever. Apart from its floor-to-ceiling graffiti decor (the authenticity of which one cannot help but doubt), the main draw here is the potential for meeting eligible single folk. If graffiti serves as a catalyst toward meeting one's mate, then more power to 'em. Frankly, the mating dance that goes on in this little hot spot is not particularly attractive. Young, single secretaries, administrative assistants, bridge-and-tunnel folk, and other equally uninteresting yuppies pack the place. Malodorous, too large, too noisy, and too boring. Let's just see Cadillac's staying power. My guess is that Cadillac Bar will end up in Edsel heaven.

CAFE DES ARTISTES
1 West 67th Street (at Central Park West)
☎ 877-3500

If there's no way you can afford to have a meal in this glorious restaurant, or at least afford to have somebody take you for one, then resort to Cafe des Artistes for drinks; for this is a New York City restaurant to be seen and experienced. Located in the heart of Manhattan's Upper West Side, Cafe des Artistes is known primarily as an upscale gourmet restaurant and is reviewed in just about every restaurant guidebook currently on the market. However, few guides make note of its bar. Tucked away in the rear corner of the restaurant, the bar is small (seating perhaps ten at the max) and cozy. Most patrons are waiting for tables, while some are catching a quick buzz between engagements. The bar, like the restaurant, is warm, romantic, and traditional, and offers a good selection of finger foods to help wash down your cocktails. It's an ideal place to take a date for a nightcap and dessert after seeing *The Nutcracker* at Lincoln Center. A blazer and slacks are appropriate, so you may opt to leave the leather pants at home. The staff is cool, professional, and well-trained. So are the patrons.

CAFE 43
147 West 43rd Street (between Broadway and Sixth Avenue)
☎ 869-4200

Sedate and pretty, Cafe 43 offers an attractive and quiet option for theater drinks. Formerly O'Neals Times Square, Cafe 43 has pretty much kept its former neo-Victorian decor. White tablecloths, candles, Tiffany lamps, white-tiled floor, high ceilings, etched glass, and overhead fans create an amiable, bright, and cheery atmosphere. The crowd at Cafe 43 tends to be on the conservative side, choosing to sit quietly and comfortably at small tables rather than stand and shout over typical restaurant din. Ideal for having an intimate conversation with a friend or for having a friendly job interview over lunch without any distraction. To feel comfortable, dress in business clothes, suitable theater attire, or other conservative and acceptable fashions. The next time you have to kill some time before curtain, you might very well sample one of their twenty-one wines served by the glass, ranging in price from $3.50 to $8.50. Try them all and you can guarantee your show will be a "smashing" success.

CAFE GRAND CENTRAL
28 Vanderbilt Avenue (in Grand Central Terminal)
☎ 883-0009

Tucked away in a corner balcony off Vanderbilt Avenue, Cafe Crand Central is one of those places you have passed a million times while running to catch a train but have probably never noticed. This smart, sophisticated, and surprisingly intimate bar and bistro located right in the heart of Grand Central Terminal offers the opportunity to "drink in" the majestic beauty of the terminal. A large square-shaped bar, located in the middle of the space, is surrounded by tiered table seating. Classical music, cool marble surfaces, and potted palms add allure. Its open airy space, complemented by rattan-backed chairs and bar stools, creates a surprising feel of being in a Parisian outdoor cafe. If you enjoy watching the parade pass you by, you will be in for quite a treat. Not only will you have a bird's-eye view of the terminal's comings and goings, but the stream of commuters dashing in and out for drinks before making the trek home should keep you occupied. At peak times, the bar can get crowded. Nevertheless, Cafe Grand Central is unexpectedly relaxed and comfortable and can make it very easy to forget about the rat race home. The crowd tends to be upscale and well-dressed—a rather interesting-looking bunch. If you're on the go, this may very well be worth the stop.

CAFE LUXEMBOURG
200 West 70th Street (between Amsterdam and West End Avenues)
☎ 873-7411

Uptown's answer to Tribeca's Odeon (*see* The Odeon) is the Cafe Luxembourg. Located in the heart of the Upper West Side, only steps away from Lincoln Center, the Luxembourg is a perfect trendy and convenient stop for after the opera or ballet, or for West Siders on their way home after the theater. A very clean and pleasing decor featuring mirrors, tiled columns, and black-and-white terrazzo floor, complemented with wonderful background music, contributes to the feeling of Paris in the thirties. But don't let it fool you—the crowd is very eighties: lots of limos and celebrities, big with the film, TV, photography, and fashion sets. Everybody looks like they could be "somebody." The dress is *très* chic—lots of black and white, trendy leather, sparkling rhinestones, and men in zoot suits. Although reservations are a must for the popular restaurant, you have to take your chances to get one of the twelve seats at the bar. There are a few small tables and chairs within the bar area; if you can manage to get one, great—but don't count on it. Most people come with their own cliques and stay pretty much to themselves. Some are waiting for tables, and some are just waiting for the big break. Although there's lots of checking out at the bar, it's mostly a matter of seeing how one is wearing one's stocking seams *this* week in New York. The staff is young, hot and smooth—lots of good bone structure. The place is hot. Go late. Who knows, isn't this where Ashford and Simpson "found the cure"?

56

CAFE MADELEINE
405 West 43rd Street (between Ninth and Tenth Avenues)
☎ **246-2993**

Pretty and French, located right next to the West Side Arts Center, Cafe Madeleine caters to off-Broadway theater folk. The brightly lit bar at the head of this pretty restaurant is a fine place to use as a rendezvous point with friends. Not particularly crowded, easygoing and comfortable, Madeleine is well suited for after-theater martinis. But under no circumstances should you stay on for dinner: The food at Madeleine is in total contrast to the surrounding physical beauty. At all costs avoid a meal here; a total throwaway. Since you can't do much to a bottle of gin, Madeleine is acceptable for a quick drinking visit. You must go to this bar with friends—otherwise you will end up talking to yourself.

CAFE SOCIETY
915 Broadway (at 21st Street)
☎ **529-8282**

And yet another showstopping yuppie pleasure palace has debuted in the trendy Lower Fifth Avenue zone. This grand stage set of a restaurant, straight out of a Busby Berkeley musical gone Oriental, makes a dazzling first impression. It simply takes your breath away. The room is soaring, graceful, and deco chic. You can imagine men with white gloves and black canes tapping their shiny patent-leather shoes down the stairs from the balcony. Massive pink-and-black-bordered square columns drive the eye up to the huge chandelier and balconied dining room and back into the soaring space. The glorious etched-glass mirror over the bar, unbleached wooden floors, black fluted chairs, and rear wall-to-wall mural are truly sights to behold. Upstairs, downstairs, at the bar, at tables, the crowd is striking. Blond women in tight black dresses partner pony-tailed men. Accessorized and groomed to the hilt, this sleek downtown artsy group consumes champagne by the magnum and thrives on late-night dining and socializing. The bar offers a large and separate area with substantial room to stand, sit, or lean against friends. Two oversized deco upholstered chairs (not unlike the ones you would expect to find in Louis B. Mayer's private screening room) provide prime gawking space in the ultimate of comfort. Cafe Society, like other upscale restaurants that offer a large bar area, attracts dressy patrons who enjoy drinking in a restaurant setting. Cafe Society's outstanding beauty offers the ultimate setting for drinks in the fast lane.

CALIENTE CAB COMPANY
61 Seventh Avenue South (at Bleecker Street)
☎ 243-8517

If the Hard Rock Cafe were to go Tex-Mex and relocate to the Village, all they'd have to do is exchange Hard Rock's Cadillac jutting out over the sidewalk with a Checker cab and throw down a sidewalk cafe. Airy, loud, and lots of fun, Caliente, one of the first in the area's Tex-Mex explosion, reigns supreme for outdoor margaritas in the Village. If you want to sit outdoors, be prepared to pay a minimum charge. However, the indoor bar is designed with plenty of room for standing and "hanging out." The crowd is young and lively. You get the feeling that you could be at a summer poolside party. Perfect for a West Village stop-off and for watching the never-ending and never-uninteresting crowd pass by.

CAMELBACK & CENTRAL
1403 Second Avenue (at 73rd Street)
☎ 249-8380

You may ask yourself, "What does this name mean and where does it come from?" Well, wonder no more: It's the name of two crossroads in the architect's hometown of Scottsdale, Arizona. The elegant, upscale interior was no doubt designed for a hipper crowd than the customers these days, who could be doing the bossa nova to the piped-in music if they still remember how. The bar itself seats about fifteen people and has a banquette behind it that is adorned on either end with a stunning floral arrangement. The brown wooden columns behind the bar have lighted front panels and look like an Oriental interpretation of art deco. Indirect lighting bounces off the bright yellow walls that are the loudest thing in this sedate establishment. The continental cuisine is exquisitely presented, but pricey. Stop by for a cognac or cappuccino and Chocolate Sin, but be advised that that's the only sin going on in here.

CAPSUOTO FRÈRES
451 Washington Street (a block south of Canal Street)
☎ 966-4900

Down and out in Tribeca-ville? This elegant, rustic French restaurant offers another downtown drinking option. Brick walls, large windows, and brass trim add warmth and charm to this very special eatery. A relatively large (and surprisingly empty) bar greets you at the entrance, but more noteworthy is the outdoor terrace with umbrella-topped tables accessible through the center of the restaurant. Go catch a sunset over the Hudson River and watch the sky light up in front of your eyes. Meet a date after work and have a heart-to-heart. Don't go to Capsuoto Frères expecting to talk to a soul; it is clear here that the crowd (as well as the service) is just a little off. Imagine a Staten Island–Queens Italian-Jewish special-occasion crowd all dressed up for a special night on the town, and you have the clientele here. Even the waiters seem to be out on the town (and to lunch).

CARAMBA!

918 Eighth Avenue (between 54th and 55th Streets)*

☎ 245-7910

The original Caramba doesn't even have a sit-down bar, but it became a popular drinking spot because it was a pioneer in the concept of moderately priced Tex-Mex food and extremely potent frozen margaritas. Although there are many such restaurants now, Caramba still packs 'em in at all its locations. The interior of each Caramba manages to reflect the ambience of its particular area, but the clientele is basically the young and the trendy, whether they're East Side preppies, West Side preppies, midtowners, or downtowners. Loud and crowded, but a good way to check the pulse of the neighborhood.

THE CARLYLE HOTEL

35 East 76th Street (at Madison Avenue)

☎ 744-1600

The Carlyle is a class act. No question. By the time your first footstep settles into the luxurious lobby carpeting, you know you are in for quite a treat. Not unlike a segment

---

*As of this writing, there are three other Carambas in New York: Caramba!!, 684 Broadway (at 3rd Street), 420-9817; Caramba!!!, 2567 Broadway (at 96th Street), 749-5055; and Caramba!!!!, 1576 Third Avenue (at 89th Street), 876-8838.

of *Lifestyles of the Rich and Famous,* the Carlyle's sedate, sophisticated, and private style has lured the truly wealthy, international, and powerful set. It would only make sense that the following two bars at the Carlyle be in a special league unto themselves.

THE CARLYLE CAFE When he's in town, the Carlyle Cafe presents the legendary Bobby Short Tuesday through Saturday nights. Two shows, ten P.M. and midnight, charge a $25 cover. However, a small elegant bar located in the rear of the room offers the option of enjoying the show for a mere $10 cover. And it may very well be worth the expense for the chance to hear Mr. Short play in this wonderful grand parlor room. If you want to get a seat at the bar, plan on arriving at least a half hour prior to curtain. Midweek shows offer better seating prospects.

BEMELMANS Located directly across the hall, Bemelmans Bar is a small hotel-lobby bar which also offers evening entertainment. The room itself is a vestige from the grand old parlor days, with frumpy gold draperies, hearty leather chairs, a battered-looking bar, and whimsical wall murals painted by artist and writer Ludwig Bemelmans, of *Madeleine* book fame. After 9:45 in the evening, a $5 music charge is in effect for jazz pianist Barbara Carroll performing at the keyboard. But aside from late-night entertainment, Bemelmans offers an interesting day and after-work option. Celebrities, hotel guests, and neighborhood "Bemelmans boys" drop by to enjoy the clublike atmosphere. Art dealers, marketing execs, and interesting and successful East Side folk share the space at the intimate ten-seater bar. Even Rex Harrison enjoys a good Bloody

Mary here. Elegant, stately, and special, the Carlyle is about as "New York" as New York can get.

CENTURY CAFE
132 West 43rd Street (between Broadway and Sixth Avenue)
☎ 398-1988

This trendy, fun, and noisy spot right off Times Square mixes heavily with the surrounding world of entertainment. It would only be natural for its decor to be appropriately theatrical. A fabulous neon movie marquee frames the long bar in this large, cavernous, pink space punctuated by a glitzy staircase and enough aspiring actors on staff to make Flo Ziegfeld blush. (At least for some, it's a gig on Broadway.) The bar here can be a jumping spot before and after theater as well as on weekends. If you are lucky to get there early enough, grab one of the cocktail tables and surround yourself with your friends. Otherwise, get into the crowd queued up at the bar, play your favorite video on a video jukebox, but be prepared to lose parts of your conversation to the noise level. In other words, this is not the place for an intimate tête-à-tête. The crowd tends to be on the young side, but the bar is also popular with an East 40s after-work crowd. Even if you have spent $45 on a ticket to some turkey that you know will fold, rather than be stranded out in the cold, warm up in this popular, hip, and attractive cafe.

CHAPITEAU RESTAURANT
105 West 13th Street (between Sixth and Seventh Avenues)
☎ 929-8833

The hottest French bistro capturing the hearts of the young and the beautiful crowd draws its front-window Levolors in order to ensure a sense of privacy and to keep "street folk" from gawking at its prized patronage. This is quite simply the rage in late-night dining. A crowd four-deep at the bar dresses in an array of styles from black T-shirts and pony tails to silk blazers to fashions still six months in the future. Tribeca art folks, fashion groupies, photo beauties, and Euro-Trash have found their new home—at least for the moment. The place itself is rather unsettling, with a hodgepodge of styles, which in no way evokes any sense of warmth or charm. It's brightly lit, with white walls, neon spotlights, floor-to-ceiling columns, and a performance area in the middle of the room to break up the surprisingly large space. Tables are extremely close to one another and the only factor ensuring any sense of privacy is the assaulting noise level. Located at the front of the restaurant, the long bar is rather straightforward, with whimsical pink neon running along its dropped ceiling. Two bassy speakers pump music directly into the bar area. The bar in this frenetic French frenzy is, as one would expect, lively; but you can't help but notice the sharp change in clientele from 8:00 to 10:30. At 8:30, an eclectic mix of nerds, women hunting for husbands, borough jewelry, and neighborhood strays dots the bar. But by 10:30, designer haircuts, pretty faces, tanned bodies, and pampered smiles emerge from streetside limos and are welcomed warmly by management. If you're not a regular here, don't even try to break through the management's "deep freeze" policy. The place is packed night after night. Chapiteau's elitism, attitude, and noise level are about as assaulting as one finds in New York. Come with friends, play "trendette," and be in *the* place to be seen. Enjoy your entrance—everyone in the immediate vicinity will check you out. Feel even better when you exit and you're on your way home.

CHELSEA PLACE
147 Eighth Avenue (between 18th and 19th Streets)
☎ **924-8413**

Enter an antique shop and browse through dusty time-pieces. Keep walking through the door of an old armoire and enter one of the most bizarre bar/restaurants in Manhattan. Over the river and through the woods, one indeed finds a bar, but when you finally do slip through the armoire, you feel like you took a wrong turn in Queens. Lovely stained glass windows from an old church in Brooklyn are illuminated by artificial lighting. But nowhere in this windowless room do you find any indication as to the time of day. All week, excluding Sundays, a pricey $10 cover is in effect for the privilege of enjoying live bar music. If live music performed by a blind organist to a dead-beat crowd is your cup of tea, then enjoy. Creepy. Far better, less expensive, perhaps less exotic options available in the immediate vicinity.

CHEVYS
27 West 20th Street (between Fifth and Sixth Avenues)
☎ **924-0205**

They're all singing "Bye-Bye Miss American Pie" past the vintage red Chevy convertible parked at the door, slurping beers and spending their week's pay on the chance to have down-home fun at this new fifties sock hop. A designer's dream of malt shop chic and 1980s discotheque succeeds in its knockout deco bar, wall posters of Marlon, Marilyn, and Dean, and toe-tapping retro music that whips this crowd into a frenzy. The space itself is large and its dance floor, front and center, is surrounded by an assortment of tables, chairs, and bar stools. Chevys attracts a young, loud, vibrant crowd bounding with a seemingly endless supply of uninhibited energy each night of the week. Boisterous, carefree, and cruisy, this boy-meets-girl crowd is sure having a swell time. Chevys draws an especially large crowd between five and eight P.M.—administrative assistants, middle managers, and yuppies-in-training all enjoying spirits and free dinner buffet. After-work cocktails fuel this crowd into what looks like a Saturday Night Fever. You'd be hard pressed to find a higher energy spot midweek. It's almost tough to believe this group is going to work the following day. The fun continues through the evening but after eight P.M. and all day Saturday, a $5 cover is in effect. Don't let weekend lines dampen your spirit. Enjoy the fraternitylike atmosphere and rediscover the football captain in you. You may very well leave with a cheerleader. Rah. Rah.

CHEZ MA TANTE

189 West 10th Street (between West 4th and Bleecker Streets)

☎ 620-0223

Wonderful French doors slide open and embrace the warm-weather breezes to gently caress you on a summer night in this petite West 10th Street bistro. Chez Ma Tante's primary business is bistro dinner, but keep this spot in mind when searching for a sophisticated Village outdoor cafe serving drinks in stylish surroundings. The rectangular room is soft and inviting with pale blue walls, oversized French posters, and brass fixtures. Choose a table that protrudes out onto the street and enjoy the steady stream of West Villagers that stroll by. Indeed you will notice that most of the neighborhood folk simply stroll by—few, if any, stop in for drinks. The spot draws a surprisingly East Side crowd, the overwhelming majority of which is here specifically for dinner. The bar itself is not particularly inviting and has only four seats packed tightly together. However, Chez Ma Tante will seat you streetside for drinks if you arrive anytime after their dinner crunch. Dress stylishly East Side and sport your favorite horn-rimmed glasses. A bit of luxe West Village sidewalk fare; rare to come by.

CHINA GRILL
60 West 53rd Street (at Sixth Avenue)
☎ 333-7788

With hard surfaces, dark walls, soaring space, suspended mushroomlike lighting fixtures, and frenetic noise level, this place is the trendiest, head-turner, midtown hot spot of the minute. Located in the middle of the entertainment industry and lodged in the ground floor of the CBS Building, China Grill cost a mere $2.4 million to open its doors and certainly seems to be entertaining an appropriately upscale, tony crowd. Its slick bar, spanning half a city block, is softened by Parisian wicker bar stools overlooking an open kitchen, where dozens of cooks turn out California-Oriental cuisine. Feeling more like a downtown Tribeca, loftlike eatery, China Grill is a splashy and spicy midtown spot to mix and mingle. Worth a gawk, a giggle, and a drink. If nothing else, enjoy the bleached-wood floor with writings by Marco Polo stenciled in green and gold.

CHUMLEY'S
86 Bedford Street (near Barrow Street)
☎ 675-4449

Having served its time as a speakeasy during prohibition, Chumley's remains unmarked and tricky to find, tending to keep away those not in the know. Find your way through a narrow courtyard; when you do, it will be well worth your while. A dark, rustic, relaxed, inexpensive, and informal pub—the mystique continues. Great place to grab a beer and burger while playing your favorites on the juke-box. Dress strictly for comfort. Nurse your hangover the following morning in front of a wonderful fireplace.

CHURCHILL'S
1277 Third Avenue (between 73rd and 74th Streets)
☎ **650-1618**

The well-worn bar is a turn-of-the-century mahogany mas-terpiece with carved wreaths and garlands and columns. Black-and-white pictures of horses and horsemen hang on the white stucco walls above a green leather banquette with tables for dining. Classic jazz fills in the background. With all the overcrowded, trendy spots in this area, the sedate thirty- and forty-year-old regulars must be glad to still have a calm and quiet place to call their own.

CIAO BELLA
1311 Third Avenue (at 75th Street)
☎ **288-2555**

The bicycle motif brings to mind the movie *Breaking Away* and its young hero's great love for all things Italian. That same love is expressed in an interior that could be straight from Milan: the postmodern tables with a wiggly red line swimming on a granite-gray top that's supported by black and red tubes, black-and-red folding chairs, a sleek, black enamel bar, and small circular ceiling lights that are white with a red rim. Waxy red high-top tennis shoes walk across the walls, and a lot of gorgeous Italian clothes, on the young, trendy, East Side crowd, walk around the crowded restaurant where the tables are neck and neck. For all its self-conscious style, this swinging scene seems to lack any substance.

CLAIRE RESTAURANT

156 Seventh Avenue (between 19th and 20th Streets)

☎ 255-1955

The Manhattan diner's fickleness is nowhere more apparent than in this Key West transplant. Riding on her Key West success, Claire decided to open a Northern sister restaurant right in the middle of Chelsea. Aided by the design folks behind the musical *Dreamgirls,* Claire built a strikingly beautiful restaurant featuring exotic tropical decor with white stained floors, navy walls, latticework, and Bahama fans. Originally, the clientele was almost exclusively gay. Then *New York* magazine ran an article praising the restaurant's wonderful fresh fish menu. Soon the mink-coat-and-limo crowd came out in droves and pushed out many of the gay patrons. But this was only for a short respite. Today, the limos and minks have moved on to trendier restaurants, and much of the original gay clientele is back in attendance. The handsome bar with snakeskin trim at the front of the restaurant still draws an interesting and attractive crowd—more men than women, and most come with friends. What's most pleasant is that the normal sexual tension associated with gay bars doesn't really operate here, making it easier to start a conversaton with a neighbor. Dress is strictly guppie—leave your Levis home. If you got caught up in the crowd that abandoned Claire, make it a point to revisit. Pretty crowd, pretty bar, slick, summery, and fun. Try it in the dead of winter and warm up in the heat of Key West.

PJ CLARKE'S
915 Third Avenue (at 55th Street)
☎ 759-1650

By now you've probably read a lot about this famous Third Avenue drinking haunt. In fact, this place is so famous that if you haven't made a visit here yet, you may not wish to admit it. This spot is definitely worth your while. If you walk by the large windows and peer into this great-looking mirrored bar with its wonderful intricate woodcarving, you can't help but think of the Marx Brothers routine where everyone is crammed into a phone booth. Like sardines in a can, the after-work crowd packs PJ Clarke's day after day, night after night, heavy on the preppie and yuppie set. The place is masculine, pubby, and clubby; you can just about smell the beer when you walk in the door. Choose a beer from their wide selection and soak up the history; this is New York pub life personified.

COLUMBUS
201 Columbus Avenue (at 69th Street)
☎ 799-8090

If you are looking for a hot spot to meet for drinks after work and must be on the Upper West Side, then as of this writing, you need search no further. This is Columbus Avenue's dress-up and "let's be an adult" hot and new trendy bar of the moment. Men in navy business suits and white starched shirts with women sporting ironed blond hair and grown-up careers mix, mingle, and gawk at the many celebrities drawn to the spot. Dark, plush, and romantic, Columbus's interior sports brick walls, red carpeting, Victorian fixtures, beamed ceilings, and a dark wood bar. What's strange here is that you could almost feel like you are in a resort hotel lobby bar. Columbus has that large and popular but not particularly warm feel to it. If you're hungry (and have access to an expense account) you might very well want to try this chichi Continental menu, although it's skewed toward the pricey side. But Columbus serves Columbus Avenue well as the newest and latest sophisticated and, at the moment, very popular bar.

COVENT GARDENS
133 West 13th Street (between Sixth and Seventh Avenues)
☎ 675-0020

Opened as an English pub in the middle of Restaurant Row on 13th Street, Covent Gardens originally courted the trendy and chic crowd with its English country charm and beauty. Lodged downstairs in a Village brownstone, the restaurant is divided into two distinct rooms—a large outer room which houses the bar and an adjacent room for the restaurant and piano. The large, rectangular bar can seat up to thirty but it is rare to find such a crowd here. The crowd which has remained after the trendy exodus some years back is a somewhat strange and dowdy neighborhood mix. But if you can disregard the crowd, you will find a relaxed and easygoing spot where one can easily nurse a beer over and beyond a comfortable time limit. Great place to have a fight with a lover on neutral territory and know that the drinks won't cost a fortune. It's quiet enough so you can hear each other, and private enough that no one else will care. It's a shame they don't move the piano into the bar. Perhaps it would liven things up a bit.

THE CUBBYHOLE
438 Hudson Street (at Morton Street)
☎ 243-9079

Reliable sources indicate that women's bars come and go. My lesbian friends report that one weekend you're in a huge room or a cramped hole in the wall with what seems like every other woman in the city, dancing in a space smaller than your feet, turning a year older on line for the bathroom, a year drier trying to get the bartender's attention. The next weekend the place is gone, or has moved on, or has a new name, but the crowd remains the same.

The Cubbyhole, however, has managed to stay the course. Its name fits its size, and on weekend nights the crowd spills into the street and the noise level inside is deafening. But it's not a bad place to meet people and to dance, and the place turns into a quiet retreat on first-of-the-week nights and early evenings. Women's sports teams that practice nearby come in after a workout and the place has its regulars. There is not much sitting space around the dance floor, but then, most of the people aren't into sitting when the jukebox is hot.

Expect typical New York City drink prices—that is, expensive. The bathrooms are usually acceptable. There is a cover most weekends and some late weeknights. Call for prices and times.

CURTAIN UP!
402 West 43rd Street (between Ninth and Tenth Avenues)
☎ 546-7272

This off-Broadway requisite, located right off Theater Row, is a perfect rendezvous point for before-theater drinks or for an after-theater supper and nightcap. Critique your theatrical experience, cruise the bar, or perhaps gander at

Leslie Uggams supping quietly in the corner after her performance. Broadway show tunes grace this warm and lively spot, which draws a typical theater crowd—a good mixture of gay and straight—actors, producors, writers, and other assorted aspirants. You can rest assured that the relaxed, friendly, and somewhat haphazard service is by actors waiting to rip their aprons off in exchange for pancake makeup and a follow spot. The bar is large and friendly—everyone is sort of "up"—thriving and surviving in the theatrical playground of New York. You can just about feel the talent. Perfect for getting the latest pulse of Broadway. Springtime adds an excellent outdoor cafe. Star Broadway drinking at off-Broadway prices.

JIMMY DAY'S

186 West 4th Street (at Barrow Street)
☎ 929-8942

This mainstream West 4th Street staple offers a perfect corner haunt serving great burgers, delicious fries, and a wide selection of draft beers. A large television screen mounted in the corner plays the latest rock videos and is used primarily by this crowd to watch sporting events. With the boisterous crowd that seems drawn to this place you can just forget about having an intimate conversation with a friend when the Jets are on the ten-yard line. Loud, spirited, and fraternal, Jimmy Day's offers a consistently good college publike feeling complete with checkered tablecloths. And if you are not into the latest sporting event, Jimmy Day's busy corner location is ideal for watching the crowds pass by. In springtime, grab a table outside and partake of the parade.

DELMONICO'S

56 Beaver Street (between William and South William Streets)

☎ **422-4747**

If at the end of a business day you want to find the so-phisticated Wall Street spot for drinks, then follow the men in Big Business suits, overcoats, and bulging brief-cases, and chances are you will be on the right path to Delmonico's. Pass through a revolving door and be greeted by the inviting charm of this Old World triangular tavern and you know you have arrived. Oak paneling associated with Wall Street boardrooms and private membership clubs, polished wooden floors, beige ceiling, and warmly lit over-head brass fixtures spell power, success and money. There is no doubt—this is serious Wall Street drinking. Formal, stately, and graceful, Delmonico's services the men who deal in stocks, options, mergers, and bull markets. And the patrons here are indeed predominantly men. The place feels more like a men's club than anything else; you will be hard pressed to see women drinking here. If there are any in the house, chances are they will either be dining in the rear room, taking a meeting at one of the cocktail tables in front, standing in very close proximity to a male escort. The large rectangular bar, reminiscent of the one used in *Cheers,* can comfortably seat forty with additional standing room for fifty. Lots of Wall Street men on expense accounts mix with brokers and analysts winding down after an active day of trading. Drinks are pricey—expect to pay $2.50 for a soda. But it may very well be worth the price for the opportunity to eavesdrop on the latest insider trad-ing scam.

DON'T TELL MAMA
343 West 46th Street (between Eighth and Ninth Avenues)
☎ 757-0788

Chances are if you're going to visit this cabaret/bar located in the heart of the theater district, you probably won't tell Mama—or better yet—don't bring Mama. A predominantly (but by no means exclusively) gay male crowd frequents this fun, friendly, and upbeat piano bar. There are two rooms, of which the front, main room is the more popular, with a long bar, plenty of tables and chairs, and lots of room to stand and croon. In the back room, a small nightclub is available for budding young talents to showcase their wares. Not only offering a convenient location for industry people, DTM provides a good performance space for the up-and-coming set. Reservations are recommended for these shows. However, the real action is in the front. A wonderful pianist whose greased fingertips seem to be dipped in a vial of speed can play any and all of your requests. He's terrific. Occasionally, a patron will step into the spotlight to perform solo, but generally this is a bar where the whole crowd can sing along—and even off-key is acceptable. The place is absolutely packed on the weekends and crowded weekday nights after theater. This is the perfect after-theater haunt. So after seeing *42nd Street,* walk those dancing feet to 46th Street, and enjoy this lullaby of Broadway.

DORAL PARK AVENUE HOTEL
70 Park Avenue (at 38th Street)
☎ 687-7050

A handsome balladeer meanders around the room with his guitar singing softly in Spanish. A green leather banquette encircles the room with tables that are a discreet distance apart. Wood-paneled walls of a rich luster open into arched windows with brocade curtains tied back at the sides. Globe lights in ornate brass fixtures are mounted on the walls and behind the small bar. Bits of overheard conversation include foreign accents discussing the Rothschilds and American accents discussing divorce settlements and Reagan's foreign policy. The clientele is older, urbane, elite, international, and the waiters in this stately room are gentlemen for whom it is a respected profession. Cosmopolitan in a sophisticated, understated way. Not for the weak of wallet.

DUKIE'S (aka GOLD BAR)
345 East 9th Street (between First and Second Avenues)
☎ no phone number

A bar with bars on its windows? Only in the far East Village would a club open and keep its window bars closed. Occupying what was once a neighborhood liquor store with its hand-painted WINES & LIQUORS sign still posted overhead, Dukie's is about as close to a stereotypical East Village club as one gets. Housed in a diminutive space, the club has the look of a neighbor's hi-tech basement, with gray walls, wood-plank floor, and makeshift bar. A silver toilet seat displayed prominently over the bar constitutes interior decoration. The club called Dukie's operates exclusively on Friday nights out of the space housing Gold Bar which, throughout the rest of the week, is a typical neighborhood spot. But on Friday nights, Gold Bar metamorphoses into a funky, hot, swinging dance club with loud disco music and a live DJ who favors well-known hits from the past. Attracting an interesting East Village ambisexual crowd, patrons gladly plunk down the $2 cover charge for the chance to dance and party in this jumping room. Where else could the music be so good, the crowd so exciting, and the price so right? Let's hope the bars on this bar will deter most folks from wandering into this surprise gem. Shh.

DUPLEX
55 Grove Street (off Seventh Avenue South)
☎ 255-5438

If Doe is a deer, a female dear, chances are she'd be found vocalizing at this Village venerable. Serving as a launching pad for such luminaries as Barbara Streisand, Joan Rivers, and Bette Midler, the Duplex takes its name quite literally and offers two distinct club rooms. Upstairs at the Duplex features a jewel-like cabaret room which presents self-contained musical and/or comedy acts that change regularly. It's a great place for new singers or comedians to showcase their talent. It's also a place for the more established yet still struggling artist to work, to polish, and to perform. Reservations are recommended for their nightly shows, and depending on the show, expect to pay $6 cover with a two-drink minimum. The crowd is here to see the particular performer, so the room tends to be warm and loving, packed with friends, family, and the occasional agent. However, it is downstairs at the Duplex where the action really is. If, on a weekend night, you're lucky enough to get in the door and down the steps to the bar, you will most certainly have the chance to drink, sing, and be merry. The downstairs bar is a quintessential sing-along Village piano bar. The room is small, cramped, low-ceilinged, brightly lit, and punctuated with Broadway posters and warm spirit. There are about nine tiny cabaret tables and chairs which seat about thirty midgets comfortably. If you're not in the bar before 9:30, you can forget about getting one of these tables. The bar is literally packed elbow-to-elbow, vocal-cord-to-vocal-cord, and after a good drink and a little "Do-re-mi," everyone starts to loosen up—singers, performers, and Wall Street brokers alike—for

everybody can relate to vintage Rodgers and Hammer-
stein. The repertory is heavy on Broadway and pop, and
within an hour you can hear anything from Alfie to Zorba.
Although predominantly under forty, the bar's crowd is
very mixed and difficult to categorize: gay, straight, bi, tri,
Village diehards, and walk-ins from West Dakota. A leather
queen singing "Oklahoma" next to a sweater-set co-ed
actually weaned in Oklahoma is not an uncommon sight.
The common draw here is that everybody gets the chance
to sing around the campfire. There is no cover or minimum
charged downstairs. Climb every mountain, ford every
stream, and follow every rainbow until you find your way
to the Duplex. It is well worth the hike.

DUSTIN'S

834 Second Avenue (between 45th and 46th Streets)
☎ **687-6360**

On the back wall of this long and narrow bar hangs a mirror
framed by small round lights, reminiscent of a dressing
room or a marquee. Toulouse-Lautrec-type posters line
the walls and the green and white checkerboard floor is a
tasteful echo of the inviting green and white exterior. The
menu offers burgers, seafood, lighter items such as salad
and quiche, and a large assortment of after-dinner coffee
drinks. Although Dustin's aspires to be a bistro, it's actually a loud and boisterous hangout for the over-thirty-
five crowd, a place where flocks of men in business suits
swoop down on a single chick in hopes of becoming instant
friends.

THE EAGLE'S NEST
142 Eleventh Avenue (at 21st Street)
☎ **691-8451**

When you're too pooped to pop, Chelsea's Eagle's Nest is not the place to hit. Loud, late, and libidinous, the Eagle's Nest has been and remains one of the city's most popular gay cruise bars. Located on the far west side of Chelsea, the Eagle's Nest caters to the hot, gymed, muscular, T-shirted, late-night partying, Levi 501 crowd who seem to have no plans for the following day, let alone the following morning. The place is virtually deserted before midnight and really starts to sizzle around two A.M. The bar is large—in fact, it is one of the largest stand-up cruise bars in Manhattan. Two long back-to-back bars divide the space into two equally large rooms. Traffic is shared with its neighbor bar, one block south, the Spike. While the Spike caters to an older crowd more into leather, the Eagle's Nest gets a younger, more diverse bunch—from East Siders in Levis to Fire Islanders to librarians. The Eagle's Nest has all the essential ingredients for a good cruise bar: it's dark, crowded, and large, with lots of places to cruise, good-looking men, a pool table, and great music with a live DJ. With this recipe, it's no wonder the place *cooks!*

EAR INN
326 Spring Street (between Hudson Street and Seventh Avenue)
☎ **226-9060**

Housed in a Federal-style house built by James Brown in 1817 on the border of Soho and Tribeca, the Ear Inn looks, feels, and smells like a "real" drinking man's bar. It is dark, shabby, and a bit on the sleazy side, but you can't help but take pleasure from the history seeping from its wood-frame rafters. Surely the metamorphosis from private home to speakeasy was not an easy one. Today the crowd drawn here is an eclectic mix: depending on the time of day, it can run the gamut from Tribeca artist cool to New Jersey truckdrivers in for a quick belt before bucking tunnel traffic. Grab a booth, have a beer, and let the good times roll. Come with a friend and bring your own fun.

ELAINE'S

1703 Second Avenue (between 88th and 89th Streets)

☎ **534-8103**

Notorious Upper East Side haunt catering to an interesting celebrity and literary crowd, i.e., Woody Allen. As far as eating is concerned, this is Woody's home away from home. One can pretty much count on seeing Woody and Mia sharing dinner in the corner and ruminating about his next "untitled" project. Overseen by the infamous Elaine (known for not being the most friendly to "outsiders"), this restaurant has become something of an insider's club over the years. Literary powerfuls, publishing giants, and Hollywood folk talk options, advances, and guarantees. The large and traditional bar in the front of the brightly lit formal and elegant dining room offers a great view of the restaurant and does fairly brisk after-work business. But the bar at Elaine's really starts going late at night, when all the interesting folk can come out to play without having to worry about being back in the office at nine A.M. Eavesdrop on your neighbor's conversation and have no doubt that you are hobnobbing with a very sophisticated New York bunch. Dress for the paparazzi.

EMPIRE DINER
210 Tenth Avenue (at 22nd Street)
☎ 243-2736

In the good old days of all-night binges, after-hour clubs, promiscuity, and good old-fashioned decadence, the Empire Diner threw open its silver deco doors to the late-night set with outstretched arms. Open a full twenty-four hours a day and serving everything from breakfast to dessert, the Empire was an immediate success, and no wonder. The designers took a genuine 1950s deco diner and refurbished it with a cool, sleek, sophisticated New York feel. It's set up like a traditional diner: a long black formica counter with matching vinyl stools runs the length of the room, with table seating along the facing windowed wall. Everything is spotless and shiny. However, muted lighting, a mirrored bar, candlelit tables, and a pianist add romance, warmth, and panache. The crowd during the week is predominantly interesting Chelsea locals; weekends tend to attract a more middle-of-the-road crowd trying something a little funky. The bar offers a surprisingly extensive wine list, ten interesting selctions of beers, and several wonderful drinks designed specifically to warm up a winter's soul. Try the delicious hot rum cider. What's funny (or rather quite sad) is that the Empire Diner has survived longer than many of the clubs it originally serviced, and unfortunately, longer than many of its former patrons as well.

ETCETERA
1470 First Avenue (between 76th and 77th Streets)
☎ 382-0122

The red neon ETC. sign has a tail that streaks across the long, slick expanse of glass like a comet. The upper level of this open, bi-level space is a dining area with neutral gray walls and postmodern light fixtures. Dinner choices include salads, pastas, and house specialties such as beef stroganoff, chicken Kiev, and veal piccata in bountiful portions. The serving hours are also generous: five P.M. till midnight; the bar is open from four P.M. till four A.M. The bar area is spacious and offers an unobstructed view of the street and sidewalk traffic. The sleek, mid-thirties, career-oriented crowd inside is every bit as much on the go.

FANELLI'S CAFE
94 Prince Street (at Mercer Street)
☎ 226-9412

A dark, neighborhood corner pub where you can sit comfortably and enjoy a burger and beer over the Sunday paper under a wall-to-wall photo gallery of boxers. Although Fanelli's offers a rather extensive pub menu, most of its arty patrons are here simply to drink. The bar crowd is filled with dates and friends, staying pretty much to themselves. It's actually a great place to rendezvous on a Saturday afternoon or to recap the weekend on a Sunday night. The crowd tends to be the over-thirty set, not terribly chic nor attractive, but more of a "real people" crowd. Neighborhood folk stop by for casual drinks and to grab a quick bite. Totally unpretentious and blue-jean casual, Fanelli's could very well be your neighborhood bar. Now all you need is the loft.

FINNEGAN'S WAKE
1361 First Avenue (at 73rd Street)
☎ 737-3664

This corner pub of white stucco and brick, topped by brown shingles and a handpainted sign, looks like it belongs on a rolling hill in Ireland. On the other side of the wooden vestibule they're serving up bangers and mash, fish and chips, steak-and-kidney pie, steaks, burgers, and a variety of sandwiches. Bucolic renderings of country life hang on lighted, green-painted squares on the wall and even the ceiling is painted a tranquil green. Unlike the wild and raucous pub of common Irish folklore, this is a sedate and peaceful refuge for the gentry.

FIVE OAKS
49 Grove Street (off Seventh Avenue South)
☎ 243-8885

If you're having a birthday and want to combine dinner with drinking, piano playing, and singing, then another Village piano bar/restaurant on Grove Street row, The Five Oaks, is the place to be. Judging from the number of times you will hear and sing "Happy Birthday" during the course of an evening, you will realize you are not alone in your choice of place to celebrate. A rather small and festive basement restaurant, Five Oaks offers a quieter, more romantic piano bar than the others on Grove Street. Featuring Marie Blakely at the piano (another Village landmark unto herself), the entertainment is mainly Marie at the piano, and her accompaniment to patrons who wish to get up to the microphone and sing. You never know what or who to expect to pick up the mike, as the talent is obviously completely dependent upon the draw of the crowd. Be prepared for a couple of clinkers—head for the hills when a cowboy who sings the sound track from the *Texas Chainsaw Massacre* takes the spotlight. The actual U-shaped bar, at the foot of the stairs, is small—seating maybe twelve, standing another twenty, but the place radiates warmth and charm from its patrons, bartenders, and staff. It's low key and neighborhoody—particularly during the week. The crowd varies according to the night of the week, but the establishment does enjoy a pretty heavy gay male patronage. But don't let this stop you, for here, the livin', singin', and drinkin' is easy. And you too can have your moment in the spotlight. This is a jewel of a bar.

FLANAGANS
1215 First Avenue (at 65th Street)
☎ 472-0300

Inside the front door is a set of saloon doors and through the slats you can see the length of the crowded bar and a stained-glass WELCOME TO FLANAGANS mural. Amber lights and pink globe lights give the bar area, which is completely segregated from the dining area, a hazy glow. Lyrical Irish accents pervade the room, and there's live Irish music nightly, with more traditional music played Wednesday through Saturday. On Monday through Friday, from four till nine P.M., all popular drinks are half price at the bar and there are complimentary hot and cold hors d'oeuvres. When the drinking age changed from eighteen to twenty-one, Flanagans changed from a rowdy beer hall to a place where young businessmen and -women could come to socialize with old friends and make new ones. Most of the effort seems directed toward making new ones, though.

FLORENT
69 Gansevoort (between Greenwich and Washington Streets)
☎ 989-5779

Truckers, meat cleavers, cobblestone streets, anonymous safe sex pits: voilà Florent. When Florent Morellet chose the meat-packing district below 14th Street for the location of his deco diner, the downtown crowd was quick to follow.

An unlisted telephone number was given to his "A" crowd, a move certain to maintain some feeling of exclusivity and guarantee a great-looking clientele. Open round the clock, Florent tends to be popular with a young trendy crowd who enjoy bistro fare at very affordable prices in an equally trendy setting. The decor is strictly diner deco—a long formica counter with adjustable vinyl stools, harsh overhead lighting, and tables crammed one on top of another. From eight o'clock on, the joint jumps with a frenetic animated energy; restless eyeballs, checking everyone out, dance around the room. Order a Manhattan at three A.M., and check the fare for a morning departure to Paris on the bulletin board overhead. Leave the chocolate cake behind—its richness will most likely have to be declared in Customs.

FORMERLY JOE'S
230 West 4th Street (at 10th Street)
☎ 242-9100

Just a stone's throw away from the hustle and bustle of Sheridan Square, street jugglers, break dancers, the infamous Tiffany Diner and the Riviera Cafe, you will find this relative newcomer to the neighborhood. Apparently having little problem holding its own, Formerly Joe's, with its long, attractive corner layout, its large bar area, restaurant, and palm-tree-lined outdoor cafe, adds a friendly and exciting voice to the neighborhood. A muted gray interior, attractive tiled floor, and deco lighting fixtures delight the eye. Accordingly, the crowd is hip, attractive, interesting; a good mixture of gay and straight, young and old, artists and businessmen. Weekdays or weekends, there always seems to be some action at the bar. Apart from pulling up a stool to do some serious drinking, you might want to indulge in fresh oysters from Joe's seafood bar with a glass of chilled champagne. But beware of weekends and the inevitable Village invasion. Consider yourself lucky to nab a place to sit. A lively, loud, and jumping weekend atmosphere lends itself to beers and good friends. An interesting alternative to glass-enclosed Seventh Avenue cafes for West Village drinking and quality bistro food.

41ST PRECINCT

24 East 41st Street (between Fifth and Madison Avenues)
☎ 679-3565

A police insignia of leaded glass hangs in each of the tall arched windows and a gigantic 41ST PRECINCT mosaic greets you as you walk in the door. Inside, the motif is continued with black and white posters of 1920s cops, rings of keys on the wall, jail bars that separate the dining room from the bar area, and waitresses who wear blue shirts with police badges. The "tempters" on the menu include an appetizer-sized pasta, soups, and crudité and dip. The huge bar area and numerous tables accommodate a large crowd that's a diverse ethnic and racial mix of young people who are happy to be calling it a day at work. Forty-first Precinct is not open on Saturday or Sunday and closes on Friday nights when the last of its customers heads out to catch the train home to Jersey or one of the outer boroughs.

FOUNTAIN CAFE

Lincoln Center Plaza (Broadway; between 64th and 65th Streets)
☎ no phone number

Prime outdoor Lincoln Center imbibing can be enjoyed in this seasonal oasis smack in the middle of Lincoln Center. Most commonly frequented by Lincoln Center folk before catching an eight-o'clock curtain or after the final curtain has rung down, the Fountain Cafe offers leisurely outdoor relaxation in the center of one of New York's most prized architectural gems. Even if you are *not* holding a pair of grand tier tickets to the Stuttgart, you can sit and enjoy cocktails right alongside the spewing fountain (providing of course that we are not in the midst of another drought). Whether or not you are scheduled to hit one of the cultural events for the evening, you will find this cafe a perfect place to sit, relax, drink, and lazily watch the throngs of well-dressed culture vultures trekking through Lincoln Center. It's hard to deny that a hot night at the opera can certainly be enhanced by enjoying a convenient and cool refreshment—only footsteps away.

4D
610 West 56th Street (at Eleventh Avenue)
☎ 247-0612

The latest club in nightlife warfare opened a "downtown" dance bar at an uptown address. But only four days after it opened, the downtown team of Frank Lynch, Cornelius Conboy, and Dennis Gattra severed relations and bowed out of the project. As a result, the original East Village-Tribeca crowd at whom the club was originally targeted has stayed away, and left a rather disappointing middle-of-the-road crowd. The interior itself is comfortably designed; a large main dance room is subdivided by recessed bars and cozy lounges, which create a sense of intimacy. The theme is moon-crater spacey and features textured walls, interesting prism-box dioramas, and special infrared lighting. Weekends are popular with guests arriving before eleven P.M. with invitations that waive the $20 admission fee. The crowd is in its thirties, successful, dressed, and somewhat reserved. You can be pretty sure that nobody gets too drunk or takes too many Quaaludes here. Make sure to leave your sneakers at home. Doormen demanding "appropriate" attire add a touch of Brooklyn tackiness and are certain to scare away any of New York's more interesting folk. Going out to dance in New York is not easy. 4D offers an option, not a terrific one, but certainly passable.

THE FOUR SEASONS

99 East 52nd Street (between Park and Lexington Avenues)

☎ **754-9494**

If you're looking for an "A-league" drinking spot where you can get dressed to the nines to start a very romantic date (or end a very late one), then you just might have your limo pull up to the Seagram Building and deposit you into the Four Seasons' lap of luxury. The entrance into the Grill Room, complete with its Miró tapestries and sculpture, is worth the price of admission alone. There is no question—this is New York's room for power lunching. Look for Kissinger, Korda, and Iacocca all having lunch together; you might just think you are at Madame Tussaud's Wax Museum. During lunch, the Grill Room cooks with film and publishing folk, who move into the Fountain Room at night. But elegant stemware and wonderful munchies are available at the bar day *and* night in the Grill Room. Every New Yorker should visit the Four Seasons at least once—even if it's just to taste their fabulous chocolate cake. The memory (and calories) will last a lifetime.

FRANK'S

431 West 14th Street (near Washington Street)

☎ **243-1349**

In the heart of sleazy meat-packing land, this small family-run spot has transformed itself into a trendy and chic nightspot. What's interesting here is that by day, Frank's caters to the butchers and meat dealers who wholesale in the area and to the truckers who carry their meats. A bloodstained apron is not a peculiar sight. But at night, the white tablecloths come out (no bloodstains), the Bentleys pull up, and hearty French food is set forth. It gets fun late at night (or real early in the morning, depending on your perspective—and career) when the limo late-nighters mix with bloody beef boys. Although the actual bar runs half the length of the room, most bar patrons drink standing up—for no other reason than that bar stools are few and far between. A strange locale to go for drinks, but well worth your while to stay on for dinner.

FRIDAY'S
1152 First Avenue (at 63rd Street)
☎ 832-8512

One of the original swinging singles bars along this First Avenue strip, Friday's is rumored to be the prototype of the bar in *Looking for Mr. Goodbar.* Although the singles scene is still alive and well here, it's tempered by a more relaxed neighborhood element, and younger and older East Siders mingle comfortably. The bar area is roomy, though often crowded, and overlooks the tables and booths of the dining area. The bar and booths are made of dark, heavy wood with brass fittings and they are softly illuminated by stained glass hanging lamps. Although the bright blue brownstone is strictly New York, the trademark uniforms of broad red and white stripes are now worn in Friday'ses throughout the country.

GINGER MAN
51 West 64th Street (east of Broadway)
☎ **724-7272**

Probably the warmest and most inviting bar in the Lincoln Center vicinity, the Ginger Man offers an inviting and attractive decor and boasts an equally attractive personality. The place is warm and pubby, with pretty browns, beiges, and earth colors; etched glass and Tiffany lamps complement an attractive clientele. The restaurant itself seems to go on forever—one charming room after another makes it possible to discover new rooms each visit. A rather small but gracious and distinctive bar area greets you at the door. If you could take away about half the crowd you would be left with an absolutely terrific bar. But a crowd it does draw, and depending upon your personality, it might be just a little too crowded, dark, and smoky for real enjoyment. It is apparent that the older, well-heeled, successful, and well-dressed crowd in attendance enjoys the hearty West Side spirit. Not only does the Ginger Man attract a large Lincoln Center clientele, but it is equally popular with the ABC News contingent. Lunch time is abuzz with the boys from the newsroom. Don't be surprised to see Peter Jennings trying to forget *World News Tonight* in a dark corner. Live entertainment, particularly enjoyable when Chris Barrett performs at the piano, completes the picture. Blue blazers and matching checkbook desired.

GOTHAM BAR AND GRILL
12 East 12th Street (between Fifth Avenue and University Place)
☎ **620-4020**

This three-star Greenwich Village restaurant is also proud to share its billing as a bar. Its post-modern interior, with soaring ceilings, stately columns, and billowy gauze lighting fixtures, is the picture of elegance. A long, striking, pink marble bar just off the entranceway runs nearly the length of the room. Two private tables at the front end of the bar offer prime spots for spying restaurant arrivals and departures as well as for watching local traffic pass by the floor-to-ceiling streetside window. When Gotham opened, the bar was on every trendy's list as a place to be seen. The young and beautiful arrived in droves. Having weathered this transient storm, Gotham's kitchen has survived by maintaining a loyal clientele. Although the lively bar scene has shifted elsewhere, Gotham's bar still offers an elegant and sophisticated option for unhurried drinks in grand surroundings. Dress is more East Side than downtown Village, with a crowd tending toward upscale, conservative "grown-ups." Go after work and conclude a business deal. Better yet, start the evening off at this romantic beauty.

GRAND HYATT HOTEL
Park Avenue at Grand Central Station (42nd Street)
☎ 883-1234

A relatively new addition to the Manhattan hotel scene, the Grand Hyatt Hotel on 42nd Street is really worth a look. The striking lobby atrium, done in marble, brass, and mirrors, featuring a show-stopping waterfall and fountain, has a twinkling, modern, and festive feel. And as far as drinks are concerned, the Hyatt offers the following three options.

First, drinks can be ordered right in the lobby from a small makeshift brass bar. Patrons can order a drink and take it with them to a seat of their own choice, or use it as a prop while wandering through the lobby. Waiting for a friend or relative with a drink in tow and listening to a live piano, bass, and sax trio is not a bad option.

SUN GARDEN The "bar" bar at the Hyatt, appropriately called Sun Garden, is designed in a glass-enclosed greenhouselike atrium. Patrons are offered a choice of drinking at a traditional square-shaped bar or at individual private tables. During an extremely busy cocktail hour, you may have to stand near the bar or put your name on a list in order to get a table. The hostess, dressed in some unfortunate Hyatt flight-attendant costume, will lead you down a long, thin balcony lined with comfortable tables, rattan chairs, and private banquettes. All seats have views of 42nd Street or of the lobby. The crowd tends to be a mixture of neighborhood businessmen conducting one last meeting before heading home, Grand Central commuters deciding to postpone their voyages, and hotel guests.

TRUMPET'S Finally, for those wishing a less frenetic and more sedate restaurantlike setting, Trumpet's restaurant, located right off the lobby, offers a smaller, darker, more wintry-type bar. Decorated in deep reds with oil paintings and small clusters of furniture, Trumpet's seems to cater to more of an out-of-town crowd. Appropriate attire is requested.

Don't turn your nose up at the sound of "Hyatt cocktail lounge." The lobby itself is worth the trip—and you may just happen to enjoy a pleasant surprise.

GRAPES
522 Columbus Avenue (at 85th Street)
☎ 362-3004

When you start hitting the fringe of the chi-chi part of the West Side, you can just about feel the neighborhood change. Perhaps it's the garbage that becomes just a wee bit more sloppy. Whatever it is, you cannot help but notice a gradual waning of yuppie life and culture. But at the northern edge of the Columbus Avenue "revival," before it's too unchic and too unyuppified, you will find one more establishment with white stucco walls, a marble bar, video monitors, scenic projections, and requisite outdoor cafe tables, with a grape motif running throughout. And yes, Grapes has managed to find its audience. Fringe yuppie, attractive neighborhood single women, and a good share of black and hispanic folk (you know, the people who just happen to share the neighborhood) frequent this Upper Columbus Avenue spot. And it's just this mixture of uptown yuppies and neighborhood folk which adds excitement and interest to Grapes. If you can manage to see past its cold, slick, high-tech interior, you might very well experience some of its neighborhood warmth. Good to go with friends.

GREAT JONES CAFE
54 Great Jones Street (off Bowery)
☎ 674-9304

The bright orange and blue exterior, marked by a simple handpainted sign denoting its name, gives you a clue what to expect inside—a simple, unadorned, down-home Cajun bar and restaurant serving no-nonsense chili burgers, Louisiana gumbo, blackened bluefish, and ribs. Dim lighting reflecting off its soft orange walls creates a comfortable East Village sleaziness. The room itself is simple and straightforward; water pipes divide table seating from the bar area, adorned with a melange of sporting artifacts: hockey sticks, autographed baseballs, and old boxing posters. East Villagers and NYU students visit Jones as their local watering hole. Dressed informally in T-shirts, cut-offs, and jeans, many young patrons seem to be on dates enjoying its moderately priced menu, drinks, or good old-fashioned jukebox playing vintage Rolling Stones. On the way out, wave to Elvis posing in the window.

GREENE STREET CAFE
101 Greene Street (between Spring and Prince Streets)
☎ 925-2415

To roll a Soho restaurant, bar, and jazz club all into a space which once housed a three-story parking garage sounds like an extremely appealing idea. Terraces and catwalks surrounding the perimeter of a thirty-foot-high room add interior design elements as exciting as the concept itself. When Greene Street first opened its doors, the crowd waiting outside certainly agreed. Even getting through on the phone was difficult. After all, a dining and entertainment club set in a spectacular space with live music was hard to beat. By now, unfortunately, Greene Street has enjoyed its heyday. It never really made it as a restaurant, nor built up a loyal bar clientele, and patrons are no longer banging down its doors. Although the trendy crowd is gone, Greene Street still offers the opportunity to hear free jazz playing in the distance while drinking in very pretty surroundings. The restaurant/bar is undeniably sleek, cool, and high-tech in feel, and offers a special and spectacular spot to go with a date. The real Soho crowd has indeed moved on, but Greene Street's beautiful and romantic interior is still very much worth a visit. Bring a date and wear "dating clothes"— even if it's just to drink in the atmosphere.

GREENSLEEVES
543 Second Avenue (at 30th Street)
☎ **725-9383**

Greensleeves is a twenty-year veteran of the Kip's Bay neighborhood, but it feels like a local English pub. From the decor, you could easily believe you're across the Atlantic. The mirror behind the bar has shamrocks painted in the corners and is flanked by a brass coat of arms; the brick walls are covered with signs for Hoffman's lager, Jameson Irish whiskey, and Bavarian beer, to name just a few. Above the bar hang several softballs, autographed by barroom champions of years gone by, and a group of regulars at the end of the bar sings a chorus of "I Believe," the song indicated on the jukebox as "most frequently played." The bar is segregated from the restaurant where they're dishing up seafood, steaks, sandwiches, a wide variety of snacks, and daily specials. The dress is casual, the atmosphere is friendly, and the price is right.

GREGORY'S
1149 First Avenue (at 63rd Street)
☎ **371-2220**

On the brick wall behind the bar hangs an oversized bugle with golden light streaming out of its horn. The piano sits right beside the bar and there are four stools at the back of it for those who really want to get into the music. The bar is small, but there are also stools lined along the wall opposite the bar. The rather sparse crowd is mostly in their thirties and forties and an eclectic blend of types. Happy hour with half-price drinks and free hors d'oeuvres lasts until eight P.M. The ceiling is black, making the room feel dim, and candles flicker on the tabletops. There's a wrap-around porch and some kind of greenery trails along the top of the sloping ceiling, but it's too dark to see what it actually is. Despite the valiant efforts of the hardworking songstress, the place never really comes to life.

THE GROVE CLUB
70 Grove Street (at Sheridan Square)
☎ 242-1408

The Grove occupies the site of the venerable Duchess, the first, oldest, and often only women's bar in the city before its sad, seedy, and dishonorably engineered demise. Insiders report that things look much the same as during the Duchess era: bar in the front, small dance floor ringed by small tables. It has a decent juke box, and the bathrooms are unremarkable (a remarkable phenomenon in a lot of bars in this city). The prices for drinks are average bar prices—for New York. There's a cover charge some late nights and most weekends, which, as of this writing, includes one drink. It can get pretty crowded, but it can also be a decent hangout early in the evening. Call to check for prices and times. The Grove must be commended for two reasons: for its history (go there to say you went) and for its survival in an environment notoriously hostile to women's bars.

In addition to the bars like The Grove and the aforementioned Cubbyhole, private production groups, such as the Tomboy Club, stage women's nights on a regular and semi-regular basis at places like the Ritz and the Saint. *WomanNews* (989-7963), a monthly New York City feminist newspaper and calendar of events, available for $1 at most newsstands and some bookstores in the East/West Village (try St. Mark's Bookstore on St. Mark's Place between 2nd and 3rd Avenues), is a good source for events, happenings, and women's nights out.

HANRATTY'S
1754 Second Avenue (between 91st and 92nd Streets)*
☎ **289-3200**

A massive brick high-rise now stands where the Ruppert brewery used to be, but across the street, hanging in a row of brownstones, is a red neon sign that lets you know they're still pouring beer on this block. Make your way through the quaint wooden vestibule, pull up a bar stool, and try to decide if you'll have a Harp, Watney's, Bass ale, or one of the other brews they have on tap. Since the mid-seventies, Hanratty's has been serving the neighbors burgers, sandwiches, and entrees for under $10, plus a Saturday and Sunday brunch for about $6. The attractive interior retains its old-fashioned white tile floor, and the forest-green walls, paneled halfway up, are tastefully decorated with oil paintings and prints. A cheerful, unpretentious haven way up on the Yupper East Side.

HARD ROCK CAFE
221 West 57th Street (near Broadway)
☎ **489-6565**

The rear end of a Cadillac car jutting out over brass-plated doors marks this landmark 57th Street hot spot. Starting as nothing less than a phenomenon for the hip, groovy, and vanguard rock scene in London, the Hard Rock's founders had little choice but to cash in and transfer their smashing formula to the United States. And where else but on New York's 57th Street and in Los Angeles's glitzy Beverly Center would such a launch succeed. A large,

---

*Hanratty's has siblings at the following locations: 732 Amsterdam Avenue (at 96th Street), 864-4224; 1410 Madison Avenue (between 97th and 98th Streets), 369-3420.

loud, cavernous, and festive space is filled with floor-to-ceiling memorabilia and serves dynamite burgers by waitresses in nurselike uniforms. When the Hard Rock first opened its 57th Street doors, the crowd was the glitzy, bisexual, bone-structured, and Euro set; a doorman admittance policy was in force. But as time has passed, the chic and the restless set has abandoned the Hard Rock, and one finds long lines of out-of-towners and teenyboppers. Now that the drinking age has been raised to twenty-one, the large bar area, which can comfortably hold one hundred bodies, is basically filled with the twenty-one-to thirty-year-old set. Strict proof of age is required. On weekend nights, it is not uncommon to see a line stretching out the door until the wee hours of the morning. If you are prepared for a relatively young clientele, bop in for a sight and sound assault—Ringo's drum and Clapton's guitar are on display to complement the astounding sound system. With beers running a reasonable $2.75, it may well be worth the trek to see Chubby Checker's boots tacked up on the wall.

HARGLO'S CAFE
974 Second Avenue (between 51st and 52nd Streets)
☎ 759-9820

Like the favorite puppy you had as a kid, Harglo's is a mixture of twelve different breeds, but the combination somehow works to create something companionable and congenial. In the back dining room, art posters hang among etched-glass sconces that light the Scotch plaid tablecloths where Cajun food is served. Harglo's also serves salads, omelettes, burgers, and entrees, and a popular weekend brunch. The separate bar area up front is roomy and serves hot and cold hors d'oeuvres from four till seven P.M. on weekdays. Photo montages of faithful customers hang above a jukebox that is stocked with the latest hits, plus a little Frank Sinatra and Tony Bennett for good measure. Drop in to watch the ball game, drink a beer, and meet the neighbors. Like the decor, the crowd is eclectic, but friendly and cheerful.

HARRY'S AT HANOVER SQUARE
1 Hanover Square (at Pearl and Stone Streets)
☎ 425-3412

Harry's at Hanover Square is another favorite watering hole for Wall Street folk and hosts a most popular and lively after-work scene. Designed with a large rectangular center bar similar to Delmonico's, Harry's lacks the formality, stateliness, and polish of that establishment. In fact, this room has an almost tattered feel to it—red tablecloths, matching red columns, unattractive overhead lighting fixtures, and a well-worn floor all look like they could use a good overhaul. If the look of Harry's has a story to tell, it's probably found in that well-worn floor. A young and decidedly mixed and friendly crowd packs this place night after night, particularly toward the end of the work week. Lively, loud, and spirited, Harry's is geared much toward Wall Street singles looking to meet other eligibles. Bankers leave their megamergers behind in the office and focus their energies on trading telephone numbers. Secretaries wanting to meet brokers and brokers trying to meet VPs is the name of the game here. It's nice to know that under those drab gray suits and matching running shoes, there's real live hormones looking to get out and party. The crowd peaks at six P.M.—everybody and their cousin makes an entrance. Add to the floor's slow demise.

HARVEY'S CHELSEA RESTAURANT

108 West 18th Street (between Sixth and Seventh Avenues)

☎ 243-5644

Tucked away in nouveau trendy high-tech lower Fifth Avenue turf, Harvey's keeps its hold as a bastion of traditionalism. Woody and publike, Harvey's feels like the kind of place where they'd film a beer commercial. While the restaurant is lodged on the second floor, hearty drinkers go about their business at many comfortable booths tucked closely and comfortably together on the ground floor as well as at the long solid bar. This is a wonderful pub to go to with friends, to grab a booth, bullshit, and beer. Yuppies, locals, and old timers fill the pub night after night. Perfect for winter drinks. Call in sick, put on your favorite Shetland, bring a good book, and spend a snowy day at Harvey's. Dream of a white Christmas and you might very well get your wish.

HEARTBREAK

179 Varick Street (at King Street)

☎ 691-2388

If you're in the mood to "rock around the clock tonight," then roll up your bobby socks and hit this downtown club. Having survived the ups and downs and ins and outs of New York club life, Heartbreak seems to be the exception to the rule in its seemingly effortless ability to draw a consistently interesting crowd. When Gotham club life offered disco music, special lighting effects, and steam rising from the floor, Heartbreak sold loud retro Chubby Checker music, a linoleum dance floor, a mini-luncheonette, and a nostalgic homage to the fifties. A bust of Elvis stands front and center atop its huge deco bar, flanked by Marilyn, James Dean, and swordfish. Aside from an illuminated

Coca-Cola bottle top, neon electric guitar, vinyl records on the wall, and kitsch Statues of Liberty, the large rectangular room is kept simple. The bar itself runs the length of the room and has plenty of bar stools and counter space, and a bun-to-bun crowd. Along the rear of the room, a soda fountain serves a selection of goodies ranging from fruit juices to grilled sandwiches to desserts and remains open all night. Drink pink champagne by the glass, devour a double cheeseburger, chug down a chocolate malt, and then, if space permits, dance your calories away. Loud music pumps away at this preppie party crowd dressed in an array from sweatshirts and jeans to button-downs and silks. Groups of friends, most in their mid-thirties, get crazy on the large central dance floor, twisting, shaking, and acting like they have just discovered rock 'n' roll. Beer drinkers feeling little inhibition twist their honeys on the dance floor while hundreds gather round to watch. Upbeat, lively, and festive, excruciating loud music makes it difficult to carry on a conversation. Cover charge varies during the week and by the hour but seems to hover around $15. Heartbreak has succeeded in capturing a moment in time and looks like it will continue "back to the future."

THE HELMSLEY PALACE HOTEL

455 Madison Avenue (between 50th and 51st Streets)

☎ 888-7000

If you can possibly erase the image of Ms. Leona's advertising campaign from your memory, you might very well try to enjoy some of her drinking establishments. The Helmsley Palace offers the following four bars on the premises, each of which offers something special for its patrons. I am pleased to report that, throughout my visits, I have yet to see "the Queen" standing guard.

HARRY'S NEW YORK BAR Downstairs, right off the lobby; Leona's down-to-earth pub. A dark, long, and romantic piano bar gets a lively and animated after-work crowd. Dark mahogany paneling, beveled-glass china cupboards, and three knockout lighting fixtures create a rather formal atmosphere. The crowd is mostly professional, with an excellent mixture of businessmen and out-of-towners staying at the hotel. Although the private curved booths are ideal for an intimate rendezvous, Harry's is more of a place to go to enjoy a bustling atmosphere. With a couple of drinks, you might even be tempted to sing along with the piano. Dress business chic, and after five P.M., gentlemen are requested to wear a jacket. This hotel lobby bar works.

GOLD ROOM For more special-occasion drinking, or for no other reason than to get a different perspective, head up and enjoy this visual and historic delight. This room is something to be seen. Right off the grand staircase, enter into the most famous room in the old Villard mansion: a hundred-year-old Roman Renaissance-style palazzo. The two-story-high vaulted gold-leaf room has walls paneled with images of musical instruments; garlands of foliage in low relief complement the highly decorative stained glass windows. Place a harpist on the north balcony and the picture of elegance is complete. Women with hairsprayed Kenneth's hairdos, men in jackets, champagne toasts fill the room. Elegant, splendid, and majestic.

THE HUNT ROOM For a darker, more pubby and elegant clublike experience without musical accompaniment, wander into the Hunt Room. Featuring specially commissioned paintings that depict turn-of-the-century English hunt scenes, this bar recreates an era of grace and charm, of noblemen and kings, and certainly has the touch of the Queen herself standing guard. Extremely attractive and comfortable, this is a room where one can settle back in noblesse and order Chivas. Gray slacks are essential; a smoking jacket preferred.

THE MADISON ROOM When you think you have had enough elegance and schmaltz rolled into one, hit the Madison Room, an elegant corner piano bar overlooking Madison Avenue. Marble pilasters and columns capped with bronze mountings flank the doorway. At each end of the room are huge fireplaces of green marble accented with onyx and antique mirrors. Candlelit tables, linen tablecloths, and a Liberace-like pianist tinkering away at the keyboard add high camp to the high Renaissance style, but enjoy this splashy and elegant corner.

The Helmsley bars are not to be missed. They're indisputably expensive; save up your pennies and share a special-occasion drink in one of Leona's splendid rooms. She might even show up sporting her Hunt Room tiara.

HOLIDAY COCKTAIL LOUNGE & RESTAURANT
75 St. Mark's Place (between Second and Third Avenues)
☎ 777-9637
If you're going to "do" St. Mark's Place, then favor this "mainstream" East Village bar. Although this is a St. Mark's

fixture, you feel like you could be drinking in an upstate New York college town; but punk haircuts, blond dye jobs, loud music, leftover Christmas lights, and an occasional redneck thrown in confirm its distinctive New York ambiance. Lots of borough kids play East Village here, but nevertheless the place is very popular. You may want to check out its 7th Street mate, The Blue & The Gold, just around the corner.

HOTEL ELYSÉE
60 East 54th Street (between Park and Lexington Avenues)
☎ **753-1066**

MONKEY BAR Smack in the middle of prime Manhattan real estate, one finds this whimsical treat hidden away in the Hotel Elysée like a well-kept secret. The room is tucked away off the lobby, and adorned by a vibrant yellow and gold jungle mural illustrating monkeys hiding in all shapes and sizes. If you're not starting to grin, then the leopard-spotted carpeting and snakeskin booths will surely slap a smile on your face. Monkey Bar's small, well-worn, L-shaped bar seats only six, but cocktail tables clustered around a piano seat most of the clientele. In the afternoon, one finds a moderately priced lunch menu with sandwiches running just a notch above neighborhood coffee shop fare. However, between the hours of 5:00 and 7:30 P.M., live music performed by an appropriately toupeed lounge pianist draws a neighborhood business crowd that shares the safari grounds with hotel residents. On Wednesday and Saturday evenings, a cover charge is in effect for live comedy. In business for over fifty-one years, Monkey Bar is a good place to try a light lunch or early drinks. Chances are if you see Monkey, you will do Monkey—and most likely more than once.

HOW'S BAYOU CAFE
355 Greenwich Street (at Harrison Street)
☎ **925-5405**

Add a summer sultry night to a hot Tribeca crowd, push open sliding glass doors, turn up the Bahama fans, let the gentle breezes flow in from the Hudson River, throw in a hint of Key West and a lotta Tex-Mex, and you can sit back and enjoy fine sidewalk cruising while sipping cool margaritas. Totally unpretentious, informal, relaxed, and better yet, inexpensive, Bayou is tailor-made for cooling out with friends at the end of a long hot weekend in an old pair of shorts and a T-shirt. Watch the street scene, nosh, drink, and gossip in the evening breeze in comfortable relaxation without having to deal with "Tribeca attitude." A light, reasonably priced menu, which features the usual Tex-Mex favorites, makes a fine complement to any of their tropical drinks. The staff is a bit strange—friendly and warm—but young and hailing more from the boroughs than the big city. But that's okay—I'll take fun, friendly, and cheap for summer, and leave chic for winter.

HUDSON BAY INN
1454 Second Avenue (at 76th Street)
☎ **861-5683**

Instead of the usual mirror behind the bar, the Hudson Bay Inn has a massive stuffed buffalo head as its centerpiece. A television glows at either end of the bar and Tiffany-type lamps gleam above the red tablecloths. Although the restaurant's name evokes visions of scallops and shrimp, they actually serve salads and sandwiches. There's a wraparound porch that offers a good view of the street and sidewalk traffic and the clientele appears to be a random sample of the passing population. Their main claim to fame here is a jukebox that features recent rockers plus the likes of Sam and Dave, Lou Christie, the Ronettes, the Young Rascals, and Dion, with and without the Belmonts.

IL PALAZZO
18 West 18th Street (between Fifth and Sixth Avenues)
☎ 924-3800

What was once Hollywood's homage to Japanese cuisine in Manhattan, courtesy of Cafe Seiyoken, has now gone Italian glitz. Ming dynasty plants, dark faux-marble columns, and oriental screens have been replaced with potted palms, pink cinder-block-like walls, unbleached wooden floors, and colorful gauzes that are draped from the ceiling parading as art. While Seiyoken had a sort of grandness to it, Il Palazzo's patina is more one of ostentation bordering on the tacky. The place doesn't feel particularly substantial, and in its desire to please the limo, designer-dress, upscale crowd, the management has opted for a design which has no more warmth or substance to it than a flimsy bus-and-truck stage set. Crowded and noisy with dressed-up folks on their best "adult" behavior. "Manhattan Babylon" straight up, with a twist—boring even before it has the chance of being exciting.

THE IMPROVISATION
358 West 44th Street (at Ninth Avenue)
☎ **765-8268**

Lines snake out the door; the young and the restless in search of a good laugh and a decent table pack this very popular Manhattan comedy showcase club. The Improvisation features new and aspiring stand-up comedians; your evening can be hit-or-miss depending upon the lineup of talent. Chances are, you'll find somebody on the lineup to your liking. If you can handle a young crowd pushing to get a good table (seating is on a first-come, first-served basis), and if you do not mind being seated bun-to-bun, a two-drink minimum, and a $5 cover, you might very well enjoy yourself and have a couple of good laughs. If what they say is true, that laughter adds to one's longevity, then book yourself in for a season's pass.

INDOCHINE
430 Lafayette Street (across from the Public Theater)
☎ **505-5111**

Noho chic, Papp's neighbor, trendy, hot, exciting, and thriving, Indochine offers another pulsating downtown spot. The restaurant, packed with the Tribeca beautiful-people set, jumps to all hours of the night serving fine Indochinese delights. The small wooden L-shaped bar greets you at the entranceway with white tiled floors, a few comfortable banquettes, and two cozy window seating areas. Most patrons at the small bar (seating eight) are awaiting tables at this very trendy eatery. But with its plush and inviting green leafy decor, the spot is wonderful for summer drinks after taking in a play at the Public. Dress is downtown chic and Marrakesh playful. Although the patrons stay strictly with their own groups, this is a fine spot to hit with a date.

Be with each other; be part of the scene. Get a comfy couch near the door and watch arriving reservations . . . chances are you'll never be bored.

INTERMEZZO
1748 Second Avenue (at 91st Street)
☎ 427-3106

It's almost impossible to believe the splendid stained-glass sign above the bar is a remnant of the previous tenant, a rock 'n' roll bar with sawdust on the floor. Intermezzo has a turn-of-the-century charm with its brick walls, pressed tin ceiling, and period prints. The tablecloths are white linen, the napkins pink linen, and tulips top the tables. It's also hard to believe the restaurant's centerpiece, a stained-glass wall that says BAKERY, doesn't house an actual bakery; it's so evocative you can almost smell the freshly baked pastries. But don't despair, there are plenty of Italian entrees under $10 to choose from and a Sunday brunch for $6.95 that includes two drinks. Although it can get crowded for dinner on the weekends, come at an off-peak hour and relax in the serenity of the surroundings. And bring along a musician friend; there's a piano in the back corner which customers are free to play if they're feeling inspired.

I TRE MERLI INC.
463 West Broadway (between Houston and Prince Streets)
☎ 254-8699

In the midst of prime Soho and West Broadway chic, one can hardly miss this new addition to the block. Aside from the dramatic decor that draws one's eye, the noise and crowd spilling out into the street surely demand attention.

With large, cavernous black ceilings and brick walls, I Tre Merli's interior is an aesthetic pleasure. Feeling like a high-tech wine cellar, this Tuscan-garagelike restaurant is divided into two spaces. Downstairs a large black bar seats about twenty-five patrons and runs the length of the dining room. Large imposing doors open in warm weather and add a feeling of airiness to the expansive, sensual room. On an upstairs balcony, a small and comfortable brick loft plays host to additional dining tables. The entire arrangement is highlighted with dramatic overhead track lighting and two oversized wine racks filled to the brim with an array of bottles guaranteed to knock your socks off. You can't help but wonder if they could possibly have this much wine in stock. Could I Tre Merli cause an alcoholic to have a complete nervous breakdown? Well, when you look at the menu, the answer is obvious—these bottles are not props. In fact, I Tre Merli offers twenty-eight different types of wine—eleven white, ten red, and seven champagnes. For those who might wish to imbibe by the glass, sixteen wines are readily available, the average glass of wine running $3.50. The crowd is Soho fun; the people, like the wines, are packed to the rafters. Wear something arty and black. Go with friends, try some new vinos, and have a blast. This place is not to be missed.

JEZEBEL
630 Ninth Avenue (at 45th Street)
☎ 582-1045

In the theater district's outfield, Frank Sinatra sings quietly in the background of this elegant restaurant featuring good old Southern cookin'. Recently redesigned, Jezebel's small bar seats only five, and functions as a spot for diners awaiting tables. But if you're lucky to time your arrival correctly, Jezebel is perfect for before-theater drinks. The decor is white and airy; Bahama fans and lace add warmth and civility to this bastion of Southern charm and gentility. Wear a seersucker suit and indulge in a delicious, but pricey, sloe gin fizz. The crowd is a mixture of New York chic, suburban matrons in for the theater, affluent blacks, and tourists. Warm, comfortable, and inviting—a bit of a walk from the theater, but well worth it. An elegant and fun summer's delight.

JUANITA'S
1309 Third Avenue (at 75th Street)
☎ 517-3800

Even on the coldest, rainiest, nastiest night of the year, plan on it being wall-to-wall bodies in here. Almost every hand, whether it's twenty-five or fifty, holds a frozen margarita or a Mexican beer. The bar itself is a configuration of marble columns with gilded tops, stained-glass panels, mirrors, wood, and lamps with a geometric stained-glass pattern. It's a loud and gaudy statement in a room of quietly conventional taste. Lamps of delicate, almost lacy etched glass are mounted on richly lustrous wooden walls, the bottom half of which are covered with a heavy brocade fabric. The wooden partition between the bar and dining area has curtains of the same fabric that are drawn to cut the noise level when it reaches a deafening roar. A wraparound porch offers quieter dining with a view of the avenue, but most people seem to prefer the view at the bar. The energy is frenetic, buzzing, young, and bursting with life. They love to be jammed up here; it's part of the appeal.

JUKE BOX NYC
304 East 39th Street (between First and Second Avenues)
☎ 685-1556

YOU MUST WEAR SHOES AT ALL TIMES, reads a sign above the dance floor, which looks like a small gymnasium complete with basketball goals on either end. Old 45s cover the top half of the walls, along with posters of Elvis and Marilyn Monroe. On the far end of the dance floor sits a DJ who does dedications and patters between songs in the best Top 40 fashion. The patrons sing along to all the songs at the top of their lungs and the DJ frequently cuts the volume so the crowd can hear itself roar. The bar is a huge oval that divides the club in half; the far side offers table service and is slightly less manic. The back wall is a tribute to the early years of Elvis and the Beatles, and stills of movies and TV shows like *I Love Lucy* and *The Mickey Mouse Club* cover other walls. A pink, purple, and red neon sculpture hangs from the ceiling, and Howdy Doody sits in a glass cage staring blankly out into the crowded room. Mounted on the walls throughout the club are brightly lit jukeboxes; Rockolas restored and resplendent in all their red, green, pink, blue, and golden neon glory. The front room is more crowded than the rush-hour IRT, and the club is always filled with people who look to be lower- and middle-echelon office workers, ranging in age from early twenties to late forties. There's a $5 cover charge; Monday, Tuesday, and Wednesday are free for ladies; and they're closed on Sunday. For over three years now they've been celebrating the nostalgia boom with the baby boomers and the atmosphere is reminiscent of the best fifties and sixties high school sock hops.

JULIUS
159 West 10th Street (at Waverly Place)
☎ **929-9672**

When the roof of one of the city's oldest gay bars collapsed several years ago, the owners didn't waste any time rebuilding and restoring the pub's interior to exactly as it was. The photographs (of which there are many), the clock that traditionally runs fifteen minutes fast, and the dust clinging to the lighting fixtures have all been restored to their proper places. Unfortunately, with management's fastidious attention to recreate the original, something very basic did change.

Julius made its mark as a Village neighborhood gay bar, where one could drop in for a beer, a cup of coffee, and even for one of the best burgers in town, dubbed the Julius Burger. Sundays were a tradition at Julius. It seemed that gay men from all over the city and its environs would pass through its wooden door at some point during the course of the day. Julius offered a warm, relaxed, friendly, non-threatening environment—and in gay bars, that's not particularly common. If old friends weren't around with whom to shoot the breeze, the chances of meeting some new ones over a Bloody Mary and a burger were pretty good. Julius attracted the preppie, *New York Times* crossword puzzle, LaCoste crowd—attractive, friendly, and neighborhoody. But for some inexplicable reason, Julius has changed. The photos are still there, the burgers are still as good as ever, and the same friendly atmosphere remains, but the crowd is gone. Although some of the neighborhood diehards do remain, the Sunday scene is certainly not what it was. Dare I speculate on why a place dies? Where have all the preppies gone? Well, it seems that with the advent of video and the chi-chi clubs of the eighties, the boys have just taken flight and left Julius in the dust—with its dust-laden chandeliers. An older, less crowded, drinking crowd has moved in. Not the spunky gay bar it once was, Julius is still a great place to go with a friend and share a fabulous burger in a back booth. Trendy bars do come and go—and who knows, by the time this review goes to print, Julius might be back again at the top of the heap. It would be well deserved.

KINGFISHER
644 Broadway (at Bleecker Street)
☎ **673-6480**

Read this review quickly. Because by the time you reach the last sentence, this club may very well have passed on to club heaven. Opening the 1st of January 1986 as a dance/nightclub adjunct to the Blue Willow Restaurant, the Kingfisher has just started to gain popularity. High vaulted ceilings, dark paneling, oriental rugs lining the walls and floors, overstuffed couches, and noble lighting fixtures deem the room fit for a queen (and not the Leona Helmsley or Truman Capote types either). Lots of well-dressed thirty-year-old yuppie types in business suits and silk dresses found their way to this Lower Broadway nightclub set amidst a San Simeon Hearst Castle–like setting. The club fits the bill as a new elegant downtown-uptown hall, where ladies and gentlemen could come dressed to play. But the management, something out of *The Rocky Horror Picture Show,* has temporarily shut down the club for alleged renovations. Whispered rumors of shady legal dealings are casting a dubious glow on this club's future. Stay tuned for future developments. We'll have to see if King Arthur continues to hold court.

KING TUT'S WAH WAH HUT
112 Avenue A (at 7th Street)
☎ 254-7772

At the moment, this bar is *so* trendy and *so* vanguard that when my friend asked a waiter to confirm the bar's name (there's no sign outside), the waiter was even reluctant to divulge this info—and this was to two of its patrons well into inebriation! The attitude one gets is: "We are so cool and hip that we don't want those who don't know how cool and hip we are to be here." Rah, rah (or wah, wah) let's hear it for East Village elitism! But, you read it here— the Hut is *the* trendy East Village bar—at least for the moment. A long, narrow, crowded bar empties into a back room set up with tables and an eclectic array of thrift-shop chairs (some straight from Grandma's kitchen). Loud retro music, electric blue walls, polka dots, punk fashions, and good haircuts predominate. Crowded. An attractive set makes this place buzz. Go—but don't *ever* admit to having read it here!

LA BIBLIOTHÈQUE
341 East 43rd Street (Between 1st and 2nd Avenues)
☎ 661-5757

The location alone is reason enough to pay a visit: on the west sits the sumptuous Tudor City, which is always worthy of a stroll, and on the east a curving staircase leads down into Ralph J. Bunche park. From its peculiar perch, La Bibliothèque affords a spectacular view of the United Nations building. If you're having cocktails in the glass-walled atrium, you get the extra bonus of a stunning, straight-on shot of the Chrysler Building. The atrium's structural beams are laced with strings of tiny white lights, which lend it a festive air. In a foyer between the atrium and main dining

113

room an elderly lady in an evening gown and tiara (no lie) sings standards and plays the piano—very well, I might add. A small bar looks into the main dining room with plush blue carpet, brick walls, and blue beams that run across the sloping ceiling. The bookcases to one side make the room feel homey and dignified at once. Saturday night is the big night here; they're closed on Sunday. The clientele is thirty and up, professional and artistic types who arrive largely in couples. A cozy, romantic spot for special occasions.

LA COLONNA

17 West 19th Street (between Fifth and Sixth Avenues)

☎ 206-8660

Another grand and elegant Chelsea restaurant with natural wooden floors and pretty pastel murals offers a small and notable bar in the foyer. Seating only eight at the small bar, with additional seating for ten at five cramped cocktail tables, La Colonna is ideal for an early-evening business meeting. Depending on how things progress, you might very well move to the dining room to continue business over dinner. Before eight P.M., the bar and restaurant are virtually deserted. So if you are looking for privacy in a rather regal setting, visit Colonna at this hour—or you might want to come back late at night for a nightcap. The entire area is so incredibly trendy, chic, and interesting now, that Colonna deserves a drink—but then you can flit off to try someplace bigger, prettier, and better. After all, the grass is always greener.

LA GAMELLE
58 Grand Street (at Greene Street)
☎ **431-6695**

Trendy and mighty and oftentimes flighty, the here-today and gone-tomorrow attitude seems to be part of the New York nightlife experience. Nothing could be a better example than trendy La Gamelle. How could the formula of French bistro playing rock music at full volume located in the heart of Soho possibly fail? In fact, the formula was so on-target that for years, crowds snaked out the door at the midnight witching hour. Black leather, multiple pierced ears (i.e., multiple earrings per each ear, no more than two ears per person, please), miniskirts, and the latest from Claude Montana. Today, the place is still jumping with loud music and a lively crowd, but not exactly at the full throttle it was three years ago. What you might check out here, however, is a very comfortable after-work scene—low key, moderately trendy, and surprisingly relaxed. A very appropriate time to enjoy the pretty bar and very French atmosphere. You should be able to land one of the tables at the front, order a beer and an appetizer, or even read the paper over a late-afternoon cup of coffee. At this time of the day, the crowd is definitely neighborhood Soho folk looking to relax and unwind. Warm and cozy, you can even share dinner with a friend at the bar. Soho, neighborhood, and French—three very good reasons to take a look.

THE LANDMARK TAVERN
626 Eleventh Avenue (at 46th Street)
☎ **757-8595**

The Landmark Tavern has been around since 1868, and literally does justice to its name. Apart from designated landmark status, the Landmark lives up to all the specs of a "tavern." A dark wood interior with a cozy fireplace plays host to the small and charming restaurant in the rear. You are greeted by its informal, relaxed, and mellow bar frequently filled with locals, theatricals, and theatergoers. Perfect for a snowy night, to hide out and warm up with a shot of cognac. And if the cognac doesn't do the trick, you can pretty much count on the Landmark's relaxed personality to provide warmth and comfort. Located in the theater district's outfield, the Landmark Tavern is a spot one can count on.

LAVIN'S

23 West 39th Street (between Fifth and Sixth Avenues)
☎ 921-1288

Garment Center cuties and West 30s businessmen grace this pretty and elegant restaurant. Brass, wood paneling, lace curtains, and marble counters add a dash of country elegance to this spot. One of Lavin's biggest attractions is that it offers its patrons wine by the bottle, by the glass, and by the sip. The most unschooled wino to the most sophisticated connoisseur can be relaxed and taste an old favorite or try something new and exotic. Although there are close to twenty selections from which to choose, including champagnes and sparkling wines, new selections are offered and updated weekly, making it easy to try something new upon each visit. You can sip wine and order appetizers at the bar or enjoy a full dinner in the stately and elegant dining room. Lavin's closes its cellar doors on weekends.

LE RELAIS
712 Madison Avenue (between 63rd and 64th Streets)
☎ 751-5108

Madison Avenue East Side French, trendy and *très populaire* with the Euro-young set, Relais enjoys an extremely busy bar business in its pretty white restaurant. The small bar at the front of the restaurant always seems to be busy, with very little space to sit, and even less to stand. In warm weather, much of the bar business spills out to the outdoor cafe, which definitely adds to the Parisian flavor. You can't help but notice all the long blond hair, rep ties, and suntans. Even Robert Redford drinks here. Definitely fun for a quick frolic, and then squeeze yourself out and head for dinner. But if you do decide to pour yourself into a table in the rear, you might be surprised at the fine cuisine.

LIMELIGHT
47 West 20th Street (at Sixth Avenue)
☎ 807-7850

How much more jaded can New Yorkers get than to buy a Chelsea church and turn it into a chic discotheque? The idea alone is enough to put a fresh flip in Mrs. Beasley's bonnet from Boise. Unfortunately, what was New York's trendiest, most talked-about, most written-about, most controversial new club to appear on the night scene is now (not unlike Chinese food, a good burp and you're hungry again) a mere flash in the pan.

When Limelight opened its doors a few years ago you would sell your soul (or at least your sister) to get in. It was strictly the "A" league, limo, pretty people crowd. The charity girls moved in; fundraisers, private parties, and society matrons shared the crowded dance floor—and for good reason—the place is just beautiful. Cozy lounges, spiral staircases, catwalks, and VIP rooms break up the space into intimate and manageable zones. Gone are the church pews from the now wonderful dance floor, but fabulous stained-glass windows, woodwork, and a spectacular pipe organ remain. Now that the "A" set has moved on to bigger and debatably better, the exclusive (please let me in and I'll throw you some coke) door policy is no longer in effect. Fifteen bucks and you're in. And obviously with the new door policy (or lack thereof), a new crowd has moved in. Today's crowd at Limelight is young, less chichi, more suburban—some Brooklyn kids, lots of couples, girls with pocketbooks, and a sprinkling of gays and mailing-list comps. But what the hell—the place is still *fun*. If you are going out to dance (which is why one chooses a disco over an ordinary bar), you will not be disappointed—for the DJ knows how to keep the crowd pleased and consistently plays dynamite music. If it's dancing and drinking you're after, Limelight is still a safe and sure bet. So what's next? Today Limelight, tomorrow St. Peter's?

THE LION'S HEAD
59 Christopher Street (off Sheridan Square)
☎ 929-0670

This Christopher Street bar celebrating its twentieth anniversary is known as a haunt for writers, editors, journalists, and publishers. Dark wood bar, jukebox, muted lighting, and walls covered with framed book covers of its patrons set the warm tone of this downstairs pub. Publish or perish, they're all here—from *Dress Gray* to *Jackie Oh!* Good bathroom graffiti affirms the eclectic literary bent of the crowd here. Home cooking and good old mashed potatoes add to this pub's quirky draw.

LOLA

30 West 22nd Street (between Fifth and Sixth Avenues)
☎ **675-6700**

If whatever Lola wanted, Lola got, it's no wonder that her new hot spot in the West 20s is simply one of the most beautiful places in town. A magnificently decorated dining room with a Caribbean-influenced kitchen, Lola has an equally attractive bar also worth checking out. From the moment you enter the elegant tiled foyer filled with fresh flowers and muted lighting, you know you are in for something special. Not a penny has been spared on decor. Fabulous hanging lighting fixtures, point spots, and wonderful artwork abound. The interior is incredibly pleasing to the eye and spirit. The bar occupies the long and narrow salmon-colored entranceway into the restaurant. The actual bar comfortably seats fifteen, and the space near the bar is equipped with many small cocktail tables, upholstered chairs, and banquettes; each table sports a shiny copper lighting fixture. On weekend nights, the bar bounces to assorted jazz combos (piano, bass, drums) performing in the front area. The crowd is hot, exciting, attractive, and very cosmo. However, this bar scene is one to sample with equally hot friends who don't mind plunking down $9 for a two-drink tab. Dress ranges from leather chic to navy blazer. A young, friendly, amenable staff is overseen by Lola herself. And, if it's late enough and slow enough, you might even get to see Lola having her supper at the end of the bar. If the richness and beauty of the place doesn't get you, hers most certainly will.

LUCY'S RESTAURANT
503 Columbus Avenue (near 84th Street)
☎ **787-3009**

Pink plastic fish match the hot shades of lipstick worn by this restaurant's young and trendy female clientele. Car services dropping off young investment bankers is common. Indeed, this Tex-Mex Upper West Side restaurant does a good job of setting its priorities: in order to get to the restaurant in the rear, one must walk through the front room, which is entirely devoted to the bar. Let's just say it looks as if the restaurant was designed as an afterthought. At any rate, the decor here is great fun, with lots of visuals. And when you are finished checking out the decor and focus in on the crowd, you can't help but feel the hormones in the air. The young, cruisy, and hot-to-trot crowd is here in full force. Definite opportunities to meet other young eligibles. To be safe, go with a friend and bop along with the crowd; you might very well find an investment banker of your very own.

DAN LYNCH BAR AND RESTAURANT
221 Second Avenue (near 13th Street)
☎ **677-0911**

This popular East Village staple offers the rare combination of live music and inexpensive drinks. Loud and crowded, Dan Lynch draws the eclectic "artist-student-jazz-street-people" set. They're all getting off on the music. A long dark bar runs the length of the room; performance space center stage. Get here early for a table. A difficult spot to talk, but lose yourself in the music. And, with a couple of beers, it's not difficult. Popular also on Sunday afternoons.

THE MAESTRO CAFE
58 West 65th Street (off Columbus Avenue)
☎ 787-5990

Just steps away from Lincoln Center and around the corner from the popular Saloon, you'll find this pretty and pink West Side spot. Catering to an upscale and less trendy market than its mainstream Columbus Avenue mates, Maestro tends to get its share of North Shore ladies in for a day at the opera. But don't let that stop you. The bar at the Maestro is comfortable, warm, and pretty, and is ideal to sit and chat in before curtain. Four very eighties video monitors rest comfortably atop the bar inviting one of your two eyeballs to watch all four monitors at once. Stop in with friends, drink, and perhaps split an appetizer or two at the bar. Fun and festive, definitely worth the stop.

MAN RAY BISTRO
169 Eighth Avenue (near 18th Street)
☎ 627-4220

Smack in the middle of Chelsea's answer to Columbus Avenue, a new French bistro has taken over the quarters formerly occupied by the restaurant L'Express. L'Express was the name given this establishment by the previous owner, who transported original deco ornaments and marble artifacts here from vintage French trains. The new owners, acknowledging that it's hard to improve upon perfection, have been smart enough to keep the interior pretty much intact, and continue the right moves to woo a trendy patronage—designer room, quality kitchen, reasonable prices. The long and narrow bar that stretches from the door to the dining room attracts a fairly substantial bar crowd apart from its restaurant clientele. Depending upon the time of day and the size of the crowd, several small booths with dark marble tables adjacent to the bar might be available for drinks. But forget getting a table during the dinner crunch—let alone being able to hear your own conversation. Despite all its beauty, marble is not exactly the warmest material; even a mild din can become excruciatingly loud. Don't come here with expectations of having an intimate conversation. Come with friends and mingle with the mixed crowd—neighborhood trendies share drinks with bridge-and-tunnel folks at the bar, each not paying attention to the other. After an evening at the nearby Joyce Theater, you'd be hard pressed to find a more striking spot.

MARIE'S CRISIS
59 Grove Street (off Seventh Avenue South)
☎ 243-9323

If you happen to be walking down Grove Street and hear what you believe to be the baritone section of the Mormon Tabernacle Choir in heat, then chances are you hit upon another Grove Street staple, Marie's Crisis. Predominantly a gay male Village sing-along bar, Marie's Crisis has the feel of somebody's seedy rec room in upstate New York. You certainly feel a long way from Manhattan. As far as piano bars go, Marie's Crisis offers the best chance for singers to sing as a group; and to sing full out, for it is rare for a soloist to perform. On weekday nights, the place is virtually deserted. Come Friday evening, the place is jumping with Broadway show tunes, Gershwin classics, ballads, and pop songs. Requests are graciously obliged by a pianist who never seems to take a break—even to go to the bathroom. The crowd is gay *mixé* (lovers, friends, and singles), warm and friendly, and enjoys a comfortably wide variance in age. If you're lucky and fight the crowds to get to the bar, a beer will run $2.75. But hold on to your hats—this is a drinking crowd. If spirits are the lubricants to one's vocal cords, then it's no wonder that at three A.M. you can hear a sonic boom. This is a fun place. Come and *sing out Louise!*

MARMALADE PARK
222 East 39th Street (between Second and Third Avenues)
☎ 687-7803

There's a long window behind the bar at Marmalade Park, and even in winter when it looks straight out at the Midtown Tunnel ramp, it's a nice change of pace from looking at the usual mirrors and bottles. In the summer you get a nice view of the tables in an outdoor courtyard that's more secluded than most in the city. Marmalade Park is housed on the ground floor of a sterile brick high rise, but it's considerably warmer inside. A wooden half-wall separates the dining area from the bar, which is loaded with crudité and dips, cheese and crackers, and peanuts. Square cutglass lamps hang over the bar and small lamps with shades are mounted on square wallpapered columns throughout the carpeted room. Marmalade Park has a popular weekend brunch and draws a lot of the thirty- and forty-year-old businesspeople and professionals in for drinks after work. It's a comfortable, friendly place to unwind, relax, and meet the neighbors.

THE MARRIOTT MARQUIS HOTEL
1535 Broadway (at 45th Street)
☎ 398-1900

Unlike many other New Yorkers, I believe that New York needed a hotel like the Marriott, particularly if we have any hopes of cleaning up Times Square. Brand-new and adding another distinctive silhouette to the New York City skyline, the Marriott is quite simply Disneyland smack in the middle of Hell's Kitchen. From its glass-enclosed spaceship elevators that whisk you through a thirty-eight-story atrium, to twinkling lights, marble floors, and flower-infested bars, the Marriott is something to be seen and experienced and offers, as one would expect, a variety of drinking options in the following three bars:

JW's The first bar you encounter off the main lobby is this quiet and sleek, brass and marble eyestopper smack in the center of the atrium. Relax on comfortable plush chairs and enjoy cocktails while listening to schmaltzy arrangements of "I Feel Pretty" on piano and violin. Large trees in big brass pots break up the space and add a sense of intimacy and privacy. Prime for atrium cruising and watching the elevators zoom to the heavens. Check out the rotating clock and enjoy the twinkling decorative lights. Lots of out-of-town businessmen with martinis and couples from Chicago.

BROADWAY LOUNGE In the rear of the lobby, overlooking broadway and Times Square neon, you hit this red and brass two-story bar that looks as if it could be a set out of *The Jetsons*. And in fact, if you want to "meet George Jetson," have a drink at this revolving bar. Lots of out-of-towners seem to get a kick out of being in a bar that moves; I suppose this presents a built-in excuse for vertigo. Although this extremely ornate bar looks as if it could serve as a group hairdryer for the Brady Bunch, the view of Times Square is really a blowout.

THE VIEW BAR Take the express elevator up to the forty-sixth floor and catch the definitive view of midtown Manhattan. As far as I'm concerned, this is the newest and most exciting view bar to hit Manhattan. Plush, modern, and mirrored, this revolving bar offers unparalleled views of midtown and its environs. Don't expect much from the decor (you will know you are in a Marriott Hotel bar), but as far as views go—this one is hard to beat. Expect a large out-of-town crowd, visiting businessmen, and gawking tourists. But what an excellent spot to bring your out-of-town guests to watch the sunset and to absorb the twinkling lights of Manhattan. Equally enjoyable for jaded New Yorkers, the View Bar offers an exciting option for pre-theater drinks or for a nightcap—particularly if you are the type who enjoys going about things in a roundabout way.

MARTELL'S
1469 Third Avenue (at 83rd Street)
☎ 861-6110

Legend has it that the self-proclaimed "Oldest Bar in Yorkville" operated as an illegal speakeasy during Prohibition. Tonight a group of boys barely the legal drinking age sit watching the ball game and sipping beers while a group of older guys are playing darts and eating parched peanuts from a large brass bowl. The bartender greets some new arrivals by name and regular customers just sign their name to their dinner checks. It's easy to forget those cozy dining rooms off to the side exist, because the front room is a world unto itself. The jukebox is a treasure trove of rock 'n' roll hits from the fifties to the eighties. Small globe lights illuminate the well-stocked bar, rust-colored walls, and original tile floor. The spacious bar seats about twenty and there are several tables sporting blue-and-white checkered tablecloths that offer bar service. When the weather allows, local white-collar workers join the neighbors to enjoy the most pleasant and popular sidewalk cafe in the area.

MAXWELL'S PLUM
1181 First Avenue (at 64th Street)
☎ 628-2100

Like an old, rich dowager, Maxwell's Plum is grandiose in a wildly overstated way; it's incredibly, even amazingly, opulent in the manner of an era gone by. The bar is a sizable wooden island on the lower level and it's divided from the tables by a wooden half-wall with a brass rail on which ornate figurines dance and pose and sit. Bottles rise in majestic rows toward a square ceiling panel of brightly colored baubles that look like lighted stones. The ceiling above the main dining area boasts a larger kaleidoscopic panel of those glass stones; it looks as if someone threw them at the ceiling until they clumped together like sticky candy. This gaudy glass motif is echoed elsewhere, in lamps and an enormous decorative object by the bar that defies description. Gigantic lamps and smaller lamps of stained glass hang from the ceiling, and gas lamps with long tongues of flame flicker lasciviously on the walls beside mirrors with etched-glass starbursts or patterns of raised bubbles. The back wall is an array of mirror framed in gold filigree, wider, flowing gold bands, then an incredibly intricate carved wooden frame of flowers and garlands and lyrical lines. Above the mirrors are delicately painted pastel maidens with flowing tresses in flowing dresses, swinging on swings and posing in a lush green landscape of trees and brooks and meadows. On the side wall is an etched-glass mirror with the same idyllic vision of ladies and gents playing harps and pipes like Pan, and beside that is a lighted, stained-glass mural with Italianate angels and cherubs. All amazingly overdone, but still it feels majestic and almost elegant. There are also a number of more intimate tables along the windows of the wraparound porch. The clientele is largely older Upper East Siders, but there's a sprinkling of faces under thirty. The bar is cozy, comfortable, and friendly, but not a pickup scene, as one might imagine. Maxwell's Plum is one of a kind and every bit as theatrical as the movie palace it used to be twenty years ago.

THE MAYFLOWER HOTEL
15 Central Park West (at 60th Street)
☎ 581-0896

THE CONSERVATORY Do the Hollywood shuffle with early-morning movie moguls in this Upper West Side home for the LA set. At night, a small and intimate bar facing Central Park offers hassle-free, quiet drinks in a pleasant hotel environment which may be just the ticket after escaping from the crowd at Lincoln Center. The atmosphere is quiet, warm, and understated. Misplaced out-of-towners with rooms up above mingle with Hollywood folk. After-work conversations are sprinkled with talk of options, weekend box-office grosses, and credits. Sun-tanned agents in from the Coast strike deals with New York directors, New York directors strike deals with LA producers, and studio executives from both coasts strike deals with soda conglomerates thirsty for their next acquisition. White bucks, blazers, and stylish long hair guarantee good service. Bring a starlet, leave a producer.

JIM McMULLEN'S
1341 Third Avenue (between 76th and 77th Streets)
☎ 861-4700

A definite crowd pleaser, Jim McMullen's is always over-flowing with the kind of folks who obviously enjoy the affluence associated with the Upper East Side. They're established, with condos at home and probably abroad, exotic winter vacations, fur coats, and maids; they've made it and they've got it made. Champagne corks pop frequently and wine flows freely. The windows and doors bear an etched-glass design that is repeated in the framed mirrors behind the bar. Massive floral arrangements adorn the bar and the cream and brick walls are studded with lamps whose shades look like white frilly glass flowers. In case you've always wondered, Jim McMullen is a former Ford model who was part owner of Harper, and who moved a few doors uptown to open his own restaurant in 1977. If you have to ask, they'll assume you don't belong here.

McSORLEY'S OLD ALE HOUSE
15 East 7th Street (just east of Cooper Union)
☎ 473-8800

This landmark, created originally as an all-male ale house in 1854, co-ed since 1970, offers some of the best ale in the city. Steeped in tradition, McSorley's clublike atmosphere—wood, leather, horses, and hearty spirit—has lots of serious beer guzzlers waiting on lines out the door, particularly on weekends. After all, it's hard to beat two mugs for only $1.75. Go. You'll think you're in a Michelob commercial.

J. G. MELON
1291 Third Avenue (at 74th Street)*
☎ 744-0585

The decor here is a meditation on melons, a virtual love song to the melon family expressed through a profusion of prints, paintings, and objets d'art. Sounds of sizzling permeate the bar because the kitchen is directly behind it; it looks a little like a wooden outhouse except that one of the walls is stained glass. The menu of burgers, steaks, salads, and sandwiches is on a chalkboard on the wall above the checkered tablecloths. With only fifteen tables, the quarters are a little cramped here, so many people choose to enjoy their dinner at the bar. The outside of the restaurant is as green as a watermelon rind, with white piping, matching planters, and a false thatched roof. It's crowded inside, but cozy and comfortable. A perennially popular spot for over fifteen years with a mixed, casual, and comfortable bunch.

METROPOLIS CAFE
31 Union Square West (at 16th Street)
☎ 675-2300

Cool white marble, high ceilings, potted palms, and a jazz trio add flavor to this new yuppie haven off Union Square. Predominantly a restaurant for the chic married and almost-married set, Metropolis sports a popular, pretty, and distinctive small bar elevated in the center of the restaurant. Under a spectacular clock, neighborhood friends (some with nose jobs and gold chains, dressed on the garish and flashy side), stand with their own. Limited seating at the

---

*There's a bigger Melon at 340 Amsterdam Avenue (at 76th Street), 874-8291.

bar makes it a stand-up, have a drink, check out the scene, and split crowd. Then again, if you wish to grab a late nightcap around closing time, you might very well find a seat and perhaps someone with whom to share it. The jazz combo, set up right off the bar, adds sophistication and panache to this slick night spot. A very pretty place that could be made a lot more appealing if they lowered the harsh overhead lighting.

METROPOLIS RESTAURANT
444 Columbus Avenue (between 81st and 82nd Streets)
☎ 769 - 4444

Striking, pretty, large, yuppie, and very West Side. The Metropolis's high ceilings, stone floors, marble columns, and black accents combine to make an architectural statement on Columbus Avenue. Weather permitting, large French doors open enabling patrons to enjoy the tradewinds blowing off the avenue. In the large and separate bar area, you can choose from many tables—indoors or out—for privacy and intimate conversation. Otherwise you can stand or sit at the equally attractive and large bar. Unfortunately, by design, the place has an interesting but harsh look which lacks any real warmth or intimacy. Take a good friend with you to help fill in this gap; otherwise stay at home and watch a good rerun.

MICHAEL'S PUB
211 East 55th Street (between Second and Third Avenues)
☎ 758-2272

If you were to call Michael's Pub and ask if they have any performances on a Sunday, they would respond with, "Oh, I'm sorry, but on Sunday we will all be in church." Upon entering the pub for the first time, you might really have doubts as to whether or not they were telling the truth. At first glance, this New York City establishment does resemble something of a cloister, with its deeply stained wood paneling, confessional-style dividers, stone floors, and hanging lighting fixtures. The overall effect is one steeped in tradition, warmth, and romance. Known primarily as a cabaret showcase, presenting talent ranging from Julie Wilson to Monday nights with Woody Allen, Michael's Pub is primarily a restaurant catering to an upscale, sophisticated, well-heeled Manhattan crowd interested in both eating and seeing a good show. There are two shows nightly. A $12.50 minimum in the dining room can be spent on drinks, dinner, or desserts. The menu is varied and not particularly pricey. However, the real find at Michael's Pub is the pub itself. Situated behind the main dining room, the bar comfortably seats twenty on stools and has five or so small tables and chairs adjacent to the bar. There is absolutely no cover or minimum in the bar area, which allows a fairly good view of the performers and excellent acoustics for listening to the show. The trick here is to arrive early to ensure a good seat at the bar— or better yet, to arrive early enough to ensure the privacy of one of the small bar tables. This is not a bar to go to with a friend to catch up on old times over vodka and ice. It is a bar to go to only if you are interested in seeing the particular show. The place virtually stops during the performance—you can hear a pin drop. It's great for listening, for holding hands and making goo-goo eyes with a date. The staff is professional, courteous, and warm, and pretty much tries to stay out of the way of its patrons. Although a draft beer will run you $3.50, you can have no problem nursing it through an entire show. This is a true New York find. Where else can you eat, drink, be merry, *and* be entertained in such a royal court for such a mere pittance?

MIKE'S AMERICAN BAR & GRILL
650 Tenth Avenue (near 46th Street)
☎ 246-4115

Just when you're sure your friends have given you the wrong address and you find yourself smack in the middle of "Slaughter on Tenth Avenue," you will find the weather-worn exterior proclaiming "Mike's Bar." Somehow you still think you are in the wrong place. Undeniably a long, long way from Kansas, you have arrived at the right neighborhood oasis in the heart of Hell's Kitchen. Perhaps from sheer relief at having made it off the street alive, the moment you set foot into Mike's, you can't help but take a deep breath and relax. Comfortably funky, Mike's publike atmosphere is simple and unadorned—tile floor, ceiling fans, overhead lighting fixtures, and small restaurant in the rear. Wall decorations ranging from a salute to the UK and its Royal Family to an October theme of ghosts and goblins change at the whim of the management. The ancient wooden bar, with vintage vinyl stools and glitter-decorated mirrors, attracts a hot neighborhood crowd, with patrons and staff mixing and mingling. "This is New York's version of *Cheers*," offered one bartender bearing an uncanny resemblance to the now defunct Shelley Long. Local actors, artists, writers, and word processors enjoy the staff as much as their cronies. Patrons are invited to send Mike's specially photographed postcard from the bar. The postcard judged by the staff to be the best written each month wins a free dinner. The winner, however, is not the writer of the card, but the person to whom the card was addressed. It's always great when a cousin from Des Moines arrives waving a free-dinner postcard which has wilted in his hand from neighborhood jitters. Plan a taxi exit.

THE MILK BAR
22 Seventh Avenue South (at Carmine Street)
☎ 675-4631

The Milk Bar has held its place in Gotham club life for quite some time. Its tiny, downstairs, space age room was quite the rage when it first opened. Designed as an intimate, selective "in" spot for the downtown crowd, Milk Bar's strict admissions policy ensured privacy and popularity with the late (as in two A.M. late) set. Grace Jones, Deborah Harry, and Madonna partied here. Lots of leather outfits, Tenaxed hair, black boots, and A-list club folk. Very hip. From the outside, you would never know this was a club. Apart from a cordoned doorway, the unmarked white brick corner building looks more like a private residence than a nightclub. And when you descend the steep flight of steps, you are surprised at just how small the space really is. Visually, the room works. Everything is done in a George Jetson Space Age motif: white walls, white floors, white shiny bar, white stools, white urinals. Overhead high-tech spotlights add color. But, as one comes to expect with this turf, the Milk Bar's original cool-cat crowd has moved on to hotter and trendier spots. Once packed with an interesting crowd (even on a cold Monday night), the place now remains relatively quiet. A doorman, cold from winter winds, searches for familiar faces. A good leather jacket and quasi-interesting look now ensures admission. Fridays and Saturdays a $10 cover is charged. Drinks at all times run a steep $5. A sizzling night spot cooling down to life at a more mainstream level.

MORTIMER'S
1057 Lexington Avenue (at 75th Street)
☎ 517-6400

Facelifts, suntans, Princeton bone structure, limos, and the Gstaad group all pour into this very popular Upper East Side haunt of the rich and lazy. Something of a star among the Upper East Side restaurant set, Mortimer's has a definite cachet, catering to a WASP, successful, and celebrity crowd. Two distinct dining rooms, whose desirability depends on the time of day, are absolutely jammed at night. The bar in the front room is long, crowded, and very busy, mostly with couples waiting to be seated for dinner—but the restaurant also has a distinctive, busy crowd of drinkers not waiting for dinner. What's interesting to observe here is that the crowd at the bar is dramatically younger than those here for dinner. Young Connecticut WASPy types who prefer to hang out in all the "right" places will find plenty of activity at this bar. The place is pretty, dark, and bistrolike, with a high noise level and a general sense of frenetic activity. Not a place for a quiet dinner and drinks. This is uptown's answer to downtown's fun: spirited, boisterous, and ideal for people-watching. But here, very few artist folk are in attendance. Many more "grown-ups." Wear your prep school tie—this is one of the trendiest university clubs around town.

MUMBLES
603 Second Avenue (at 33rd Street)*
☎ **889-0750**

There's a football game on the television, but classic jazz on the stereo, and the jukebox ranges from Glenn Miller to the Temptations to the Pet Shop Boys. The crowd is equally varied, but casual and comfortable. Fresh flowers adorn the bar, which is softly illuminated by hanging lamps of scalloped green glass, and the bottles at each end of the bar are encased in cabinets with stained-glass windows. The bar seats about eighteen people and offers specials including nachos, fried zucchini, or fried calamari. The menu features salads, pasta, burgers, and a $6.95 brunch from noon till four on Saturday and Sunday. The atmosphere is pleasant and informal, the food is surprisingly inexpensive. The cozy wooden window seat is the perfect place to enjoy a leisurely cocktail after you've purchased your ticket for one of the many movie theaters in the 34th Street area.

MUSEUM CAFE
366 Columbus Avenue (at 77th Street)
☎ **799-0150**

On Columbus Avenue's "Freeway of Fun," across from the Museum of Natural History, resides this warm and comfortable refuge. This cafe always seems to do brisk business, regardless of the time of day, or time of year. The dining tables are strategically placed in a sidewalk enclosure making it easy to eat and drink and still be part of the avenue. For serious drinkers not wishing to wash

---

*Mumbles has brothers at 1491 Second Avenue (at 78th Street), 772-8817, and at 1623 Third Avenue (at 91st Street), 427-4355.

down their beverage with any tempting comestible, the interior bar is warm and inviting and never so crowded that you cannot sip a drink slowly while finishing off a good novel. A fine place to take yourself to write all those postcards to your out-of-town friends after the museum. While the restaurant crowd tends to be sophisticated, attractive, and very West Side, the bar crowd can be wonderfully eclectic. A museum matron sitting a bar stool away from a New Jersey truck driver is not an uncommon sight. And the real nice thing here is that both parties are made to feel equally at home.

NELL'S
246 West 14th Street (between Seventh and Eighth Avenues)
☎ 675-1567

The young and the beautiful arrive in limousines, decked in European clothes, and are ushered in past the roped-off entranceway. Fame, fortune, or a great pair of tits might allow entry. Nell's, the club that Odeon owners Keith McNally and Lynn Wagenknecht opened with cult figure Nell Campbell (Little Nell in *The Rocky Horror Picture Show*) as hostess, has been quite simply the rage in haute New York nightlife. Nell presides over her lounge in black gowns and glides about her parlors like a madam in a Victorian whorehouse. You feel as if you are in some grand old house: the two-story club features an upstairs jazz salon with crystal chandeliers, dark oil paintings, oriental rugs, polished wooden floors, and fin-de-siècle accoutrements. Lots of overstuffed armchairs and couches provide private conversation pits. The area downstairs is divided into two lounges. One has the feel of an English country mansion—green walls, velvet drapes, paintings of horses. The other room is really rather plain—beige walls, bleached floors and a few wall lamps set the stage for dancing to reggae, Brazilian funk, and Madonna. Great space and sound system for dancing. The crowd is very chichi, dressed to the nines, and enjoys this soft and exclusive addition to New York club life. You'll love it and you'll hate it—it's fun, trendy, sophisticated, exciting, boring, and pretentious. Brings back the excitement of Studio 54 days. Don't plan any early breakfast meetings the next morning. Chances are even lunch will be hard to swallow.

THE NEW DEAL
152 Spring Street (between West Broadway and Wooster Street)
☎ **431-3663**

The New Deal in Soho, formerly the WPA, offers all the prerequisites of a great bar: prime location, a pretty, dark, romantic interior, rich desserts, and live piano entertainment. Unfortunately, the New Deal clearly delivers a raw deal to its patrons. Crowded, noisy, tables packed entirely too close together, poor service, and mediocre baked goods all add to the disappointment. It is obvious that the Soho crowd has figured all of this out and has moved on to different watering holes. The crowd now in attendance is skewed more toward borough folk and misplaced Upper East Siders. Even the beautiful wall-to-wall thirties murals and live piano music Wednesday through Sunday nights just don't make up for all of the drawbacks. Pretty, but pass.

NIGHT BIRDS RESTAURANT & BAR
92 Second Avenue (near 5th Street)
☎ **254-4747**

When you've had it with loud music and standing on your feet, and you're ready for a break—it's time to hit Night Birds. Here, you'll have the chance to sit in comfort and either refamiliarize yourself with your date, or get to know the person you may have picked up earlier that evening. This low-key spot, owned by the same people who manage the trendy eatery 103 Second Avenue (across the street), offers reasonably priced drinks, a light menu, local art, and the opportunity to converse without shouting. Perfect to hit before heading home, to collect your senses (and leftover dollars), and enjoy a nightcap in comfort. Relax. You deserve it.

NIRVANA CLUB ONE ATOP THE GREAT WHITE WAY BANGLADESH INDIA PAKISTAN INTERNATIONAL GOURMET RESTAURANT & DISCOTHEQUE

1 Times Square Plaza

☎ 486-6868

Say it three times fast, or call information for their phone number—just for the fun of it. What more can one say? Schizophrenic club life atop Times Square is exemplified by this latest foray into nightlife. By day, Indian cuisine is served amidst a dramatic setting atop the Allied Building, the celebrated home of the New Year's Eve ball. But by night, Nirvana goes rock 'n' roll and rolls out a sound system strong enough to lift Gandhi out of his grave. This place is strange. At eleven P.M., dark-skinned Indian waiters scurry with dishes of curried chicken for the yuppie clientele who seem to get pleasure from having their insides rocked, rolled, *and* fed. (For some reason, curry and rock 'n' roll is not exactly my idea of soup and sandwich.) Later in the evening, white trash waitresses parading in punjab costumes join Indian waiters and hustle drinks to the rocker set. Yes, this place is truly as funny as it sounds. But forgetting the food and outrageously loud music, the room itself is a visual delight. Large floor-to-ceiling windows frame four sides of an elongated rectangular room with breathtaking views of midtown. White drapes cover the walls and ceiling punctuated by an occasional meditation cushion whimsically suspended from the ceiling. A quieter bar, decorated with mirrored fabrics popular with the elephant set, offers a refuge. The crowd comes to hear the band of their choice, and varies depending on the group performing that evening. If you can manage to scrape up an extra pair of earplugs, this might be a fun spot to drag an out-of-town guest for a drink after theater when a bit of New York decadence is called for. Don't think of going solo. Briefly *ooh* and *aah* at the sights atop Times Square, then quickly vanish on a magic carpet right out the door.

NORTH RIVER BAR
145 Hudson Street (between Hubert and Hudson Streets)
☎ 226-9411

Finally a bar that plays the kind of music you attend weddings for—and you don't have to stop at Tiffany's for a gift. Located a stone's throw away from the Holland Tunnel, this undiscovered step-back-in-time is just what the doctor ordered for nightlife ennui. Designed like an old-fashioned dance hall, not unlike the one portrayed in *They Shoot Horses, Don't They,* North River's live swing band works this crowd into a sweat Wednesday, Friday, and Saturday nights. The bar bears the original name of the Hudson River—i.e., the North River—and a large wall map illustrating the river's heritage shares the space with a pool table, jukebox, mini-bowling game, video monitor, and wooden booth seating. The room itself is fairly large, with dull yellow walls and a dark paint-chipped ceiling with overhead fans. A large free-floating bar borders on the tacky with martini graphics, Naugahyde stools, and, wherever there was a design doubt, mirrors. The focus is clearly on the Dick Clark bandstand and on the duos partner-dancing their cares away on the well-worn dance floor. From the twist to the Lindy, from toe-crunchers to Arthur

139

Murray grads, this crowd is having a swell time beboppin' to some of the best music in town. Dressed in everything from old prom dresses to blue jeans, this is not your typical Tribeca crowd; many a New Jerseyite decked in polyester finery shares the floor. Just look at the bartender's beauty-parlor hairdo and you'll know this is not exactly the tony crowd. However, united in a common pursuit, the pub draws a healthy mixture of young and old New Yorkers alike. Wear your most comfortable dance shoes and bring your favorite Ginger Rogers date. The live music is an absolute delight and creates a festive bounce guaranteed to smack a smile onto your face. It's a welcome change when the doorman taking your $5 cover (which includes one free drink) is more interested in the baseball score on his radio than in the designer label inside your suit. By "Shaking the Blues Away" you can get "In the Mood" for a "Moonlight Serenade."

NOVOTEL WINE BISTRO
226 West 52nd Street (at Broadway)
☎ 315-0100

Perhaps one of the best views of Times Square and the theater district is atop the French-owned hotel, Novotel. The lobby, set seven stories above Broadway, offers a relaxing and comfortable retreat from Times Square and is home to the Wine Bistro. Modern, quiet, and glass-enclosed, tucked away in the far corner of the lobby, the Wine Bistro offers one of the better wine-by-the-glass selections in midtown. A relaxed and somewhat romantic setting with plush comfortable chairs and a wonderful pianist complement their menu. Two dozen wines are served by the glass at competitive prices, from $2.50 for a five-ounce sample of the 1984 Beaujolais-Villages from Bouchard Père et Fils, to $12 for the luxury label of Dom

Ruinart champagnes, the Blanc de Blanc. To help wash down the bubbly, the bistro also offers terrines, duck liver, cheeses, and tartines. For a glass of wine, a slice of pâté, and a taste of Times Square, the Wine Bistro is *magnifique*. Sample a new wine. *Salut!*

THE ODEON

145 West Broadway (at Thomas Street)
☎ 233-0507

One of the original trailblazers in this very hot and now gentrified Tribeca neighborhood, the Odeon is still alive and well and very much booming. A reconverted 1950s cafeteria retaining its cool crisp deco interior, Odeon offers sophisticated dining, excellent food, late night supper, fine service, and a wonderful bar to boot. Catering to the "fast" crowd—lots of fashion people, photographers, artists, celebrities, celebrity hangers-on, and the uptown limo crowd—the place definitely has panache. Running the width of the restaurant, the bar comfortably seats twenty on stools and offers nine cocktail tables and chairs in the spacious bar area. Stand, sip, and mingle at the bar, amid the generally quite friendly, attractive, and interesting crowd, or stake out a table with some friends for some serious business. It's a perfect place to go with friends for a celebration. The festive interior and taped fifties music inspire the sipping of champagne from long-stemmed flutes. Wear something fun. Something retro is perfect. Black leather is safe. Check out the Odeon for New Year's Eve. While its restaurant patrons are enjoying a $150 prix-fixe dinner, being entertained by a live swing band, one can easily slip into the bar and welcome the New Year in high style. From its start as a mere trendy downtown eatery, the Odeon has become something of a New York staple; I am pleased to report that its reputation is very well deserved.

OLD TOWN BAR & RESTAURANT
45 East 18th Street (between Broadway and Park Avenue South)
☎ 473-8874

Established in 1897, this old, folksy, pretension-free bar is a cross between O'Neill's *The Iceman Cometh* and a Prague coffeehouse. In a neighborhood that is swiftly changing from light manufacturing to trendy design, publishing, and PR firms, this bar has held its own and refuses to give in to the chic and yuppie surrounding glamour. An old blinking beer sign, a cranky old owner, and a hand-printed QUICHE NOT SERVED HERE notice attests to the anti-yuppie atmosphere. A large L-shaped bar seating twenty, eating stalls, and plain wooden tables constitute decor. Wrangler jeans, sweatshirts, and Fruit of the Loom T-shirts mix well with slightly wrinkled khaki pants, non-Italian leather jackets, and slightly frayed traditional tweed jackets. The place gets crowded at lunch and after work, making it noisy, smoky, and filled with lightness and fun. Rolling Rock rules here. One is not serious here—particularly given the leaden hamburgers, chili, and the proud announcement that "the coffee is only four hours old." Old Times are really here, and hopefully for a bit.

O'LUNNEY'S
915 Second Avenue (near 48th Street)
☎ 751-5470

A dreary neighborhood spot which by day attracts an older down-and-out crowd slowly chewing on overcooked hamburgers and reading yesterday's newspapers. A typical Irish corner bar. By night, however, a younger shit-kicking, beer-drinking crowd appears in Wrangler jeans and cowboy boots to hear some good old country music. And if country music is your kind of scene, then it's nice to know that O'Lunney's features live country music every single night of the week. Although there is no cover charge at the shabby ten-seater bar complete with hanging glass ale mugs, seating at the tables draped in requisite red-checkered tablecloths will add a $4 music charge. Attitude, trendiness, or designer pants are simply not tolerated. A domestic beer will run $2.50. Yahoo.

O'NEALS
60 West 57th Street (at Sixth Avenue)
☎ 399-2361

Another O'Neal brother hot spot that continues to pack them in day and night is this very stylish 57th Street eatery. If you're just too Bergdorfed and Bendeled out and need a quick pick-me-up (and very possibly a quick pickup), then pour yourself into this popular bar and grill. Tiled floors, wood paneling, and etched glass add character and flavor to a seemingly bland and unexciting veneer. The draw here is obviously the crowd—lots of entertainment folk, from network executives to studio gals, all in stylish outfits and well-coiffed hair. The bar is lively and friendly with a substantial amount of cruising, particularly during the after-work "witching" hour. If you can handle the crowds (most likely you won't have a chance to sit) and feel comfortable with the mover-and-shaker scene, then O'Neals might very well be the right option. And if any producers are reading—everyone knows, you like to keep track of all your options.

ONE FIFTH

1 Fifth Avenue (at 8th Street)

☎ 260-3434

What was once home to the trendy-and-beautiful-people set has mellowed over the years to become a dependable class act catering to a traditional Village and yuppie clientele. The interior, designed to give the feel of the grand salon of a transatlantic ocean liner, is really quite glorious. In fact, much of the decor has been rescued from the SS *Caronia*, which unfortunately found its way to the bottom of the sea in 1974. The long, narrow, pretty bar attracts a lively after-work crowd of neighborhood yuppies returning after a day at the office, NYU students, art-gallery patrons, and other assorted locals. What's attractive about this bar is that many One Fifth patrons are here just for drinks with no intention of proceeding into the dining room for dinner. And late at night, One Fifth offers live music to help ease down those martinis. White, deco, slick, and special, One Fifth has weathered its initial trendiness and refuses to sink. It is still very much afloat and worth the trip up the gangplank.

ONE IF BY LAND

17 Barrow Street (near Seventh Avenue)

☎ 228-0822

Bars for a special-occasion drink in the Village are few and far between. One If by Land is certainly one to experience. Tucked away in a reconverted carriage house on Barrow Street, One If by Land's recently redone interior should be on your must-see list. A romantic, country-elegant room with exposed brick walls, two blazing fireplaces, and upstairs loft sparkles with twinkling candlelight, spotless crystal, and crisp linen. Elegant and formal, expensive and

144

dressy, the small bar off the main foyer plays host predominantly to diners awaiting tables. Don't let that intimidate you, however—sit right down and make yourself at home. This place is warm, romantic, and special; the shiny Steinway grand is the whipped cream on the cake. Pick a quiet snowy night in Manhattan and impress a date with an elegant nightcap. The stage is set for romance; bring your favorite supporting player.

THE OYSTER BAR
Grand Central Terminal
(42nd Street between Lexington and Park Avenues)
☎ 490-6650

The Oyster Bar was obviously an elegant showcase in its day, but that day has long since passed. The vaulted ceiling of beige and white parquet tiles descends into dramatic columns and the arches between are lined with strings of tiny white lights. Around the wooden bar area they have erected a rust-colored canopy that stands about eight feet from the ground. The intention is obviously to lend an intimate atmosphere to the bar, but it's poorly executed and a bad idea because the majestic ceiling is by far the best feature of the place. Pretzels, peanuts, and oyster crackers sit on the bar and on numerous small tables in the bar area. Oysters and clams on the half shell are available and can be mixed in any amount. To one side of the bar is a large, open dining room with red and white checkered tablecloths. On the other side is a dining area with rows of winding counters with stools. Past this area is a saloon with a separate dining room and bar, but it feels like a suburban seafood restaurant. The Oyster Bar is open from 11:30 A.M. until 10:30 P.M. and is closed on Saturday and Sunday. Although most of the patrons might never come here if it weren't in Grand Central Station, the workers of all ages and types who make the daily commute are grateful for the cheery comfort it affords before the long trip home each night.

PALIO

151 West 51st Street (between Sixth and Seventh Avenues)

☎ 245-4850

A "grown-up," dress-up, expense-account crowd mobs this recent addition to upscale dining in Manhattan. Lodged in the new Equitable building, Palio boasts a striking bar-and-restaurant duplex setup: an entire ground floor is devoted to the bar, and an easy elevator ride to the second floor reveals a traditional dining room. The bar at Palio is quite a knockout. The square two-story room that houses it has been designed with a sense of sophistication, panache, and style. A large semicircular marble bar complemented by black Italian modern bar stools stands center stage. Cocktail tables line the perimeter of the airy, theatrical space. It is Palio's "Sistine Chapel," however, that makes the most dramatic design statement. A bright, four-walled mural shouts for your immediate attention. The mural alone is worth the price of admission. As far as the crowd goes, Palio draws a large after-work executive bunch dashing in with mink-draped wives before running to the theater. In fact, the place virtually empties out by eight P.M. The service, indisputably pretentious at times, can be hit-or-miss. I was not particularly happy to receive somebody else's bill, but was thrilled at receiving their change. Who knows—maybe you won't even get a bill at all. With these prices, keep your mouth shut and head right for the door. Oh, but don't forget your mink.

PALLADIUM

126 East 14th Street (between Third and Fourth Avenues)

☎ 473-7171

If love means never having to say you're sorry, then Stevie Rubell's Palladium is the ultimate penitence for his financial fiasco at Studio 54. Seemingly blessed with the Midas touch, Mr. Rubell created one of the world's most exclusive playgrounds for the rich and famous (not to mention the drug infested) in the old Ed Sullivan theater in the early 70's. Yes, even Robin Leach was inpressed—for "getting in" was even better than "getting it up." Now, a decade later and a prison term smarter, Mr. Rubell and his partner Ian Schrager have put their heads together and dreamed up the ingredients for the quintessential New York dance palace of the eighties: spend all the money you possibly have left sans lawyers' fees; metamorphose the seediest, hugest 14th Street rock hall available; fly in an "Oriental design influence"; incorporate art as part of disco or at least make disco become part of art; mix a little sixties psychedelia with some eighties new wave boring video; lay the world's largest dance floor complete with gimmicky sets and revolving curtains; add enough lighting effects to give the New York Planetarium a run for its money; and throw in a little Grace Jones and a lot of Calvin Klein; and *bam*—what have you got—the look of an eighties cha-cha palace on the isle of Manhattan.

Undeniably the most oversized nightclub ever to hit the New York scene, Palladium is truly one of a kind. From the entrance, up the glitzy Las Vegas-lit stairway into the main room that appears to know no boundaires, the Palladium is a spectacular sight to be seen and experienced; a true feast for the senses. Unfortunately, with all its overscaled grandness and its desire to please all, it lacks the intimacy, warmth, and feeling of "specialness" that Studio 54 so rightly possessed. It's *so* big and *so* huge and *so* vacuumlike that you get the feeling you're in a football stadium and everyone is looking for where they parked their car. People seem to be floating around—looking like they know where they are going, but haven't found it quite yet. There are bars upstairs, downstairs, spiral staircases, bleachers, catwalks, and balconies to explore. And, of course, there is the perfunctory VIP lounge and the Michael Todd room for special receptions. Although the crowd is quite mixed, this is not a bar to go to with the idea of meeting someone. Don't even think about it. Go with friends and plan on staying with your friends. Everyone is in their own world. Don't fight it. If you don't have one, start your own brave new world. You can expect to pay $15 for the privilege of "getting in" and $4 for every beer thereafter. However, if you're lucky you'll be on the mailing list and the admit fee will be lowered to a mere $10. The best view is atop the second bar heading up toward bleacher heaven. From there you can really feel like an outsider looking in. At 4 A.M., close your eyes and click your heels together three times and you might very well get your wish.

PALSSONS

158 West 72nd Street (between Broadway and Columbus Avenue)
☎ 362-2590

One of the surprising hot tickets on the Broadway circuit is at this off-off Broadway à la 72nd Street bar which presented the musical revue *Forbidden Broadway*. This satire of the Broadway theater received rave reviews in the papers and on television and has actually lasted longer than some of the material it satirizes. A well-written, well-acted, and completely enjoyable show is presented in this intimate West Side supper club. You can reserve a table by calling in advance, but be prepared to spend a $14 to $19 cover and a $10 food or drink minimum. If you just want to catch the show, you may get a seat at the bar (first come, first served) for $10 and deal with a $5 minimum. The entertainment is clearly worth the money; the memories and laughs will stay with you for some time to come. You may want to check out the bar downstairs at Palssons if you wish to linger over drinks after the performance and still feel part of the Broadway spirit. No cover or minimum applies. At Palssons, let *them* entertain you—and undoubtedly, you'll have a real good time.

PANAMA CITY
1572 First Avenue (between 81st and 82nd Streets)
☎ 288-0999

Pink Flamingos roost in the front windows, and you can also order one from the densely populated bar (cognac, strawberries, and passion fruit). Perhaps you feel more like a Panamamama (strawberries, cream, and amaretto), or maybe you're up for an Orlando Orgy (five kinds of liquor). They also concoct a Cocoa Beach that's guaranteed to make you dream of Jeannie. Mermaids, seahorses, Florida pennants, stuffed dolphins, and Miami Dolphin plaques hang on the aquatic green, peachy pink, and sunshine yellow walls. After a drink or two you begin to sense the rolling ocean waves in the ceiling of green corrugated tin. The front wall features an immense mural starring a flamingo and an alligator that looks a lot like the one riding around on many of the shirtfronts. The crowd is young with a surprising number of girl groups out for a night on the town. The menu is a toss-up between Tex-Mex and Southern Cajun, and even the beer list conforms: Tecate, Rolling Rock, Dos Equis, Dixie, and Panama. Panama City tries hard to be tacky, but the mentality is too far uptown. The jukebox blares the Pet Shop Boys' "Let's Make Lots of Money," and that's the name of that tune. See ya later, alligator.

PANCHO & LEFTY

206 East 50th Street (between Second and Third Avenues)

☎ **319-4700**

Next door to the Crystal Pavilion, and every bit as gaudy, is the pink neon sign for Pancho & Lefty. A horseshoe-shaped bar, built of glass brick with a marble top, sits like a tiny island in front of the large window in the front dining room. The walls are lit neon blue and there are oversized interior columns, one of which blooms into a gigantic flower. The patrons, mostly in their thirties and forties, look like they just put in a twelve-hour day at the office. Named after a country-and-western song, Pancho & Lefty is just another Tex-Mex bar and restaurant. Just what New York needs.

PARKER MERIDIEN HOTEL

118 West 57th Street (between Sixth and Seventh Avenues)

☎ **245-5000**

BAR MONTPARNASSE An extremely popular bar for New York businessmen and tourists, located right in the lobby of the popular French-owned Parker Meridien Hotel. The bar is divided into two sections. A large and rather nondescript outer room has many comfortable tables and offers a great view of comings and goings, arrivals and departures, and general lobby frenetics. Under a beautiful tapestry, a pianist adds a festive and romantic touch to the room. Off of this room, you find the second part of this bar, which has a completely different atmosphere and feel. A cool, sleek, and sophisticated gray and marble bar complemented with etched glass graces the room. Relaxed, and closer in feel to a real New York bar than the outer room, here you will see businessmen comfortably reading the *Times* and sipping soda water from their very own old-fashioned soda bottles while waiting for their next meeting. The crowd tends to be older and more established. Due to its location, the bar attracts a lot of entertainment folk. An interesting mixture of out-of-towners and jaded New Yorkers works well here. Dress in appropriate hotel chic and come to play on an appropriate hotel expense account. If you favor the pricey and Parisian, you'll fit right in.

PARK LANE HOTEL
36 Central Park South (between Fifth And Sixth Avenues)
☎ 371-4000

One would think that this majestic Central Park South hotel, home of the power breakfast, would host an equally special bar. But I'm sorry to report that the bar at the Park Lane is a disappointment. The long, narrow room, dimly lit with imitation gaslights and plush bar stools, seems lacking. You feel like you are in a hotel bar somewhere in West Dakota. If there is something special or unique about this bar, I have certainly missed it. The crowd is predominantly out-of-towners and hotel guests all gawking at the intended elegance of the bar. Hotel bars work when out-of-towners mix and mingle with natives. In this case, the natives have decided to stay away.

PETE'S TAVERN
129 East 18th Street (at Irving Place)
☎ 473-7676

Known as a favorite watering hole for O. Henry and as the site where he allegedly penned "The Gift of the Magi,"

Pete's Tavern is filled with O. Henry memorabilia steeped in rich period atmosphere—brick walls, tiled floor, checkered tablecloths, muted lighting, and beamed ceiling. It is the sign over the bar advising how to live in New York on $15 a week, with an immediate $8 taken off the top for a whiskey allowance, that gives a better clue to Pete's Tavern. This corner haunt is filled with locals, friends, family, and passersby who just happen to like to drink. Preppies, hippies, young- and old-timers alike share the fratlike, relaxed, pubby atmosphere. Come prepared for some heavy drinkers and for a noisy night out on the town. Even nicer when you can enjoy the outdoor cafe.

PETROSSIAN
182 West 58th Street (at Seventh Avenue)
☎ 245-2214

The "night they invented champagne," Hermione Gingold must have had this spot in mind. This chic corner spot right off 57th Street and around the corner from Carnegie Hall caters to the champagne and caviar set who can afford to spend their family's fortune on the "good stuff." The room itself is surprisingly small, with striking etched-glass mirrors and deco artifacts, lit with a wonderful romantic warmth. The bar itself is equally attractive with high-backed black chairs, most of which are usually unoccupied, and offers a sophisticated, sleek option for intimate drinks after seeing Liza sing "New York, New York" at Carnegie Hall. Dress strictly for success—haute couture, Armani ties, crocodile handbags. Excellent for special occasions and festive drinking. Order champagne by the glass. Toast another year gone by. Welcome the New Year with elegance and style.

THE OAK BAR News anchormen, power drinkers, Saudi sheiks, tourists, and Fifth Avenue matrons share the space in this venerable New York establishment. At perhaps one of New York's most picturesque corners, Central Park South and Fifth Avenue, the Plaza Hotel, home of the Oak Bar, is a very legend in its own right. Entire books have been written or set here, movies shot here, and even presidents sleep here. If the Plaza *is* New York, then a visit to the Oak Bar is imperative. The large, darkly paneled, clublike room overlooking Central Park is—in one word— glorious. The bar itself is quite small—seating maybe fifteen at the max—but the entire room is set up with many comfortable tables and chairs, and it is here where the real drinking takes place. Most people come here for drinks with friends, business associates, family, and lovers. Across the board, the crowd is well-heeled: mink coats, Gucci shopping bags, Paul Stuart suits, and lots of Cartier. The *real* thing. Lots of the ladies stop in after a strenuous Fifth Avenue spree and a quick clip at Kenneth's for a not-so-quick belt. Nobody said shopping was easy. Ideally located in prime Manhattan, the Oak Bar is New York sophistication at its best. Close a business deal. Make a date. Celebrate an anniversary. The Oak Bar *is* a tradition— and it has certainly aged well—for each year, as it adds another ring to its trunk, it seems to get better and better.

OYSTER BAR AT THE PLAZA Tucked away in a corner of the Plaza Hotel, the Oyster Bar specializes in fresh fish and has a surprisingly large, quiet, comfortable horseshoe-shaped bar ideal for ducking into for intimate drinks. You can relax knowing that you will not have to deal with crowds, trendiness, or "attitude" in this neo-Victorian room. What's interesting here is that although you are smack in the center of Manhattan, the sense of calm makes it seem you could be miles from Metropolitan Babylon. But mistake it not, for indeed the Plaza is the Plaza, and home for some is just around the corner and up the stairs. Worth a peek.

PRINCE STREET BAR & RESTAURANT
125 Prince Street (at Wooster Street)
☎ 228-8130

Prince Street Bar & Restaurant suffers from an identity crisis. Physically, Prince Street is almost a stereotyped Soho pub: long, brown and yellow, lots of plants, earthy and Soho arty, with plain wooden tables, hard chairs, pinball games, and a local community bulletin board. This functional artsy Soho retreat was originally designed for local artists to hang out in and "share" art. But as everyone is aware, the art crowd, or at least the "real" artist crowd, has long since moved out of the neighborhood; therefore this "real artist" bar has been left without any "real artist" clientele. Prince Street remains as a kind of ghost-town neighborhood bar that in its heyday was incredibly successful and fun, but that has gotten lost in the art world exodus. Despite it all, Prince Street still offers a comfortable and relaxed Soho atmosphere where one can linger over the Sunday paper and enjoy a good burger and beer. Wear your favorite sweatpants, preferably stained with paint, and you will be welcomed with open arms.

PRIVATE EYES INC.
12 West 21st Street (off Fifth Avenue)
☎ 206-7770

What's black and white and trendy all over, shows nonstop video on multileveled screens, charges a cover, and has a different crowd for every night of the week? If it's not Bloomingdale's main floor, then it must be the video emporium in Chelsea: Private Eyes. An airy, three-barred, clean white high-tech space with video monitors from floor to ceiling, complete with a good sound system, small dance floor, and hip Manhattan crowd, make this bar a must-see. Depending upon the day of the week, the crowd will vary. Wednesday and Sunday nights are gay, Tuesday nights are frequently reserved invitational/promotional parties, and the rest of the week is up for grabs. Aside from a cover that can run as steep as $10, drinks are pricey—a beer will run $4. But on the "trendy" nights, the crowd is definitely a good-looking one: lots of Tenax, leather skirts, 57th Street haircuts, and attitude. The focal point here is on quality video—continuous, loud, interesting, and varied—from MTV to original montages. People generally come with friends but there is a fair amount of looking and shopping. Between the video, the dancing, the bar talk, and cruising, there's enough going on here to keep even the most jaded New York eyes occupied.

PROVENCE
38 MacDougal Street (near Spring Street)
☎ 475-7500

Even famed food critic Gael Greene can't get enough. One of the bright new stars to have risen on the scene this past year, Provence's lively French bistro specializing in regional fare is packing them in. Saffron-colored walls, warm wood paneling, fresh flowers, crisp white tablecloths, and shiny crystal are complemented by muted overhead lighting. Attracting wealthy East Side art dealers, established West Side lawyers, downtown dilettantes, and Richard Gere; book a table well in advance. However, even if you have secured a reservation, chances are you will pass some time at the bar waiting for your table. The handsome wooden bar adorned solely by a spotless gold-framed mirror offers an excellent view of the front dining room as well as the street, through the large front windows. But be warned: very few customers come here only for drinks, and those diners who have been "exiled" to the bar for more than ten minutes will often take umbrage. Keep Provence in mind for late-afternoon or early-evening informal and relaxed drinks. Bring postcards from the neighborhood Soho card shop, or bring a close friend to soak up the French color. In this appealing, attractive, and affordable establishment, with appetizers as wonderful as the entrees, you may feel propelled to join the throngs heading on for dinner. *Bon appétit.*

PUFFY'S
81 Hudson Street (at Harrison Street)
☎ **766-9159**

If you're down and out in Tribeca-ville, you might fall into this dark and dingy neighborhood spot. Puffy's original crowd of Tribeca loft folk seems to have got lost in the shuffle of new hot spots opening up in this part of town. Shabby and looking on the run-down side of things, Puffy's is attracting a younger and more budget-conscious patron. Lots of NYU students and borough folk shoot the breeze at the bar, drink beer, and hang out in front of the television set usually tuned to the latest sporting event. Dress is strictly blue jeans; wear your most mellow mood and you'll feel right at home.

QUATORZE
240 West 14th Street (between Eighth and Ninth Avenues)
☎ **206-7006**

In the midst of Little Spain, Robbins clothing outlets, and the Salvation Army on 14th Street, a small, smart, and comfortable French restaurant opened a few years back garnering critical acclaim. Quatorze, French for *Fourteen*, sports a long and narrow bistro layout complemented by a tiled floor and Parisian cane chairs. You are greeted by a small, charming bar, well proportioned to the rest of the restaurant. The bar is generally filled with diners waiting for tables, but a few "outsiders" are simply there for drinks, particularly late at night. It's actually a wonderful bar to hit on the way home after the theater, ballet, or even after dinner at another restaurant. To blend in with the crowd, dress in appropriate restaurant chic. Taste a delicious martini made by a man the movies would typecast as a typical 1950s New York bartender, and indulge yourself with a side order of oysters. A late-night supper at the bar is totally acceptable, *très français* and *très romantique*. A bit of French chic in the midst of 14th Street sleaze.

THE RAINBOW GRILL
30 Rockefeller Plaza (Fifth Avenue at 49th Street)
☎ **632-5100**

Somewhere over Rockefeller Center, perched atop the RCA Building, there's a rainbow worth visiting. Recently reopened with enough fanfare to set any publicist into multiple orgasm, the bar area, referred to as The Grill, offers spectacular views of Manhattan in about as swank and sophisticated a setting as you can get in New York. The doors of your express elevator to the 65th floor open onto a space lined with columns of alternating mahogany and translucent glass lit from behind. Your attention is drawn to a formal reception desk, which directs guests into one of the four dining areas: the bar and cocktail lounge, the Rainbow Room proper with its round dance floor, and two other smaller statement dining rooms. Opened as a private club with astronomical yearly membership dues, The Grill is the only room open to the public. Conceived as a kind of stage set, everything from the decor of the individual rooms to the spiffy staff uniforms to the stylish place settings come together in a harmonious 1930s style. All that's missing is Fred Astaire. The bar area itself, quite long and narrow, wraps around the south side of the building, and is decorated with warm leather furniture, deep red carpeting, and a model of a red and black ocean liner designed by Norman Bel Geddes is hung over the curving mahogany bar. Floor-to-ceiling windows offering unobstructed views of midtown and environs put Manhattan in the palm of your hand—reach out and touch the Empire State Building, see the QE2 pass the Statue of Liberty. Take a deep breath and enjoy the lightness in your head in this romantic and festive aerie with its comfortably spaced tables. Bring a special friend. Cocktails run $6.50, a light menu is available, and proper attire (shirt and tie for men) is requested. But for the privilege of drinking where the bluebirds are, that's where you'll find me.

RAOUL'S

180 Prince Street (between West Broadway and Sixth Avenue)

☎ 674-0708

Stylish haircuts, black dresses, and Armani suits fill this very pretty and hot little Soho restaurant. A terrific 1950s-looking bar takes center stage in the front room of this restaurant, which spills over into more intimate quarters in the rear. The place has the feel of a 1960s French black-

and-white "art" film; large mirrors, framed French posters, overhead fans, tiled floor, and wonderful mood music add to the panache, elegance, and warmth. Light cream-colored walls and a dark brown tin ceiling have seen the likes of many celebrities; even Lauren Hutton's legs have been spotted at the bar. The crowd is interesting, attractive, and upscale, and attracts the typical Odeon clientele. Come with friends and enjoy the atmosphere. Friendly bartenders who actually make Blood Marys from scratch are well worth the pricey tab.

RASCALS
1286 First Avenue (at 69th Street)*
☎ 734-2862

The exterior of long gray planks and white globe lights looks more like it belongs in the suburbs than in uptown Manhattan. The interior is rustic, with raw brick walls, hanging plants in wooden windowframes, red and white checkered tablecloths, and plain wooden floors covered with sawdust. There are a couple of large barrels of parched peanuts; half those shells end up on the floor along with the sawdust. The wooden bar with tile inlays is a large oval with seating all the way around, but still it's elbow-to-elbow in this popular neighborhood spot. There's lots of singles action at the bar, but the numerous tables are filled mostly with well-dressed couples in their mid-twenties or thirties. That's not surprising when you consider that the minimum age is twenty-five and proper attire is required. There are television sets hanging at either end of the restaurant and there's always some sporting event tuned in. The newer Rascals downtown is such a popular sports

*The downtown Rascals is located at 12 East 22nd Street (between Park Avenue South and Broadway), 420-1777.

bar that the New York Mets' first baseman Keith Hernandez celebrated his thirty-third birthday there.

JIMMY RAY'S
729 Eighth Avenue (near 46th Street)
☎ 246-8562

Jimmy Ray's is like a college bar for theater folk. Chorus boys, chorus girls, budding young directors, writers, and dancers meet and use this Eighth Avenue pub for food, drink, sustenance, and serious business. The unassuming entrance on Eighth Avenue, with its chalkboard memo announcing the reasonably priced specials for the evening, attracts a heavy show-biz clientele. With a menu priced to meet the demands of a young thespian's budget, it is rare to find an empty seat in the house. The crowd is predominantly young, and working or looking for work in the industry. Script readings, audition leads, coaching, coaxing, and the latest backstage gossip are exchanged in this informal and easygoing pub. If you are in the theater district and looking for an insider's place to grab a light supper and a quick drink, this is definitely the ticket. It's equally attractive late at night when the chorus kids saunter in and unwind in the comfort of "home." Jeans, leg warmers, and dance bags are particularly welcomed.

RECTANGLES
159 Second Avenue (at 10th Street)
☎ 677-8410

Keep this corner spot in mind when your thirst demands a beer with an international flavor. Located in prime East Village turf, this corner establishment has gone from neighborhood coffee shop to neighborhood coffeehouse, boasting over fifty beers from around the world. The blue-walled interior is stark with large floor-to-ceiling windows, tiled floor, and several coffee shop tables. Not exactly the picture of warmth, nor the spot to linger over drinks. The local artwork displayed on the walls tries to soften the room's edge. The draw here is the outdoor cafe, which offers a splendid view of St. Mark's Church. Twelve small tables painted in bright reds, blues, and yellows are prime for watching Astor Place haircuts pass. Try an Israeli beer. Look toward Avenue A and see bombed-out Beirut.

REGENCY HOTEL LOUNGE
540 Park Avenue (at 61st Street)
☎ 759-4100

When in town, Hollywood power folk "take drinks" in the company of rich and powerful Euro-Americans in this splendid Park Avenue hotel lounge. This is the "A Team" all right, no question about it. Established wealth and inherited money share this small and elegant piano lounge. Cream-colored walls, ritzy chandeliers, and red French/Japanese murals add elegance and warmth to this plush little hot spot. During cocktail hour, one must expect a wait to be seated. And indeed, this is a "table" bar where presidents and CEOs escort their mink-draped and face-lifted wives. Few people sit at the small bar. An extremely professional staff knows how to cater to a crowd that likes to be pampered—and apparently the crowd here is happy. The clientele tends to be older, apparently very successful, and wears the latest from Cartier. Listen for how many times Gstaad comes up in a conversation. Order champagne and have the limo waiting. Expect to pay to play. This is the big time.

REGENT EAST
204 East 58th Street (off Third Avenue)
☎ 355-9465

Jerry Herman's *La Cage Aux Folles* piano medley, three-piece traditional suits, yuppies, and graying executives share the cruising ground of this Bloomingdale's retreat. Conveniently located in midtown and extremely popular with an after-work crowd, the Regent East caters to the older, professional, successful, New York business set. The sign requesting "proper attire" at the door sets the tone. This is a "gentleman's" gay bar—no sawdust on the floor here, only Gucci attaché cases and Bergdorf shopping bags (and even these you have to check). Formality and success are in the air—Paul Stewart suits and button-down collars abound. A pianist, located in the rear of the bar, creates a festive atmosphere by leading the crowd (most of whom are in some state of inebriation) through Broadway scores and other pop tunes—many with bastardized lyrics. The staff, warm and courteous to its regulars, can be outright nasty and patronizing to newcomers. A V&T will run $2.25 at all times of the day—there are no happy hour specials. But don't let the staff ruin a potentially good time. For if "you are what you are," you might very well find "what you want" before heading out into the night.

RICK'S 181 LOUNGE
181 Eighth Avenue (near 19th Street)
☎ 691-9845

The gentrification of Chelsea's Eighth Avenue strip is certainly giving Columbus Avenue a run for its money. Rick's Lounge, a trailblazing hot spot in the neighborhood, offers stylish drinks, Tex-Mex food, prime sidewalk cruising, and a dramatic fifties interior complemented with a white grand piano. Loud music, punk haircuts, and an exceedingly young crowd keep this place thriving. Great margaritas, interesting side orders of Tex-Mex foods, and a large selection of Mexican beers will easily keep you satisfied. If you can handle the NYU crowd inside, you will certainly enjoy the Chelsea parade passing by outside. Good for late-night drinks, good music, and song.

RITZ CARLTON HOTEL
112 Central Park South (between Sixth and Seventh Avenues)
☎ 664-7700

THE JOCKEY CLUB Serious businessmen in rep ties, vast expense accounts, weary out-of-towners lodging at the Ritz Carlton, and power dating. Elegant, traditional, and understated, the wonderful bar at the Jockey Club is definitely worth checking out. Although its prevalent horsey and WASPy traditionalism might be intimidating to some initially, get over it, order yourself a martini, loosen your tie, and let yourself relax in this wonderful genteel bar located right in the heart of the Central Park South strip. This is a definite dress-up or special-occasion restaurant where ladies and gentlemen are indeed "appropriately attired": a perfect place to meet a date before dinner for elegant and quiet drinks. Sit at the very comfortable bar or choose from several tables set up in the popular front foyer. Make it your point to check out the bathroom. This is absolutely one of the most beautiful country-chic bathrooms in town. And what's even better is that you don't have to deal with an attendant standing in your way. Enjoy it. The whole place is a class act. Expect to pay class prices. Worth every penny.

RIVER CAFE
1 Water Street (Brooklyn)
☎ 718-522-5200

Although for some New Yorkers going to Brooklyn is the same as taking a trip upstate, the trek to the foothills of Brooklyn—Brooklyn Heights—is well worth the trip. A subway stop from Wall Street, an invigorating walk over the Brooklyn Bridge, or a short cab ride, and you're out of Manhattan and into Brooklyn Heights, a picturesque upscale yuppie neighborhood appealing to the Wall Street financial "buy-'em-and-sell-'em" crowd. Apart from breathtaking views from the Promenade, cobblestone streets, and affordable housing, Brooklyn Heights is the proud home of the world-renowned River Cafe.

Housed on a barge at the foot of the Brooklyn Bridge, the River Cafe's crisp and clean nautical decor offers a setting that cannot be beat. Rated, reviewed, and debated among gourmets, gourmands, and critics, the River Cafe offers unparalleled views of Manhattan and true splendor, by day or by night. Reservations are taken weeks in advance for the restaurant, but the informality of being able to just drop in for drinks makes the bar attractive. The bar is small and elegant and offers the same sensational view of the city, and needless to say, won't cost you a fraction of what it would cost for dinner. In the spring and summer, there's even an outdoor patio where one can imbibe and enjoy the cool breezes of the East River. River Cafe is a perfect place to go for romantic drinks and intimate conversation while enjoying the sunset over Manhattan. It's even the right choice to impress your out-of-town guests with the beauty of New York. A piano in the bar area adds additional panache to the twinkling lights of Manhattan. Do it—sink or swim—bring your lover, or your loved ones, and make it for drinks at the River Cafe. Don't be left ashore.

RIVERRUN CAFE

176 Franklin Street (between Hudson and Greenwich Streets)

☎ **966-3894**

One of the first spots to open its doors prior to rapid gentrification, this Tribeca bar and restaurant obviously filled a void. Vanguard residents needed a local place to hang out, to meet one another, to check the pulse of their neighborhood. What amounts to a neighborhood corner bar (although it's actually located in the middle of the block) seems now to have run its course; most likely it has suffered from the surrounding surplus of trendy eateries. One can still stop in and read the large public bulletin board, read a book at the bar, or grab a booth in the rear for a light snack or meal. The nondescript bar, however, with seven wooden chairs which seem to go unoccupied most of the time, doesn't look particularly inviting. Perhaps the locals got wind of things, took the pulse of the area, and, not liking what they saw, decided to head out into the wild blue yonder. Watch out, Astoria.

RIVIERA CAFE

225 West 4th Street (off Sheridan Square)

☎ **242-8732**

This West Village landmark is best known for its prime location, and as a strategic vantage point for watching the parade go by. Pretend you're in a sidewalk cafe in Paris; you couldn't pick a better spot to view the latest spring fashions. A relaxed, low-key atmosphere makes watching the girls go by all the more pleasurable. And if you're hungry, something on Riviera's menu should suit your palate. Every New Yorker who's visited the Village has been here at least once. Fun place. You make it what you want.

THE ROOSEVELT HOTEL
45 East 45th Street (between Madison and Vanderbilt Avenues)
☎ 687-1860

CRAWDADDY Ceiling fans spin lazily, green plants hang in front of the windows with the crawdaddy-shaped *C* of leaded glass and sheer white curtains below. The walls are glossy white, the ceiling green pressed tin with light fixtures that look like grandma's best cut-glass salad bowl. Soft jazz hums melodically in the background and the net effect is one of gentility and tranquility. It does get a big after-work crowd, however, especially guys in ties who drop in for a quick drink before heading over to Grand Central. There's plenty of room for everyone, though: the front room offers numerous intimate tables, the bar itself is spacious, and a separate oyster bar sits between the bar and the back dining rooms where they're serving New Orleans cuisine. Crawdaddy is open only for breakfast and lunch on the weekends. Drop in at an off-peak hour, for this is a bastion of comfort in a rather inhospitable area. Makes you want to order a mint julep and dream about the green, green grass of home.

ROUND'S
303 East 53rd Street (between Second and Third Avenues)
☎ 593-0807

If the cloud of the gay plague has not yet rained on your parade, and you're still up and ready, and ready to *pay* for action, then you just might try this East 53rd Street establishment. Yes, this New York hustler hot spot is something of an institution in and of itself. In every city there's some sleazy bar tucked away which one frequents knowing that it is going to cost to play. Imagine what New York's primo-ballerino hustler bar would have to look like: that's right—go for broke—lots of slick mirrors, designer bar, plush banquettes, a baby grand piano, a lounge singer, more mirrors, and even a restaurant. Anything to cover up the underlying sleaze. With all the opulent trappings here, it's hard to believe that the bottom line in this joint is that *money talks*. The crowd is one-third hustler, one-third out-of-towners, and one-third older gay power and wealth (yes, of course, your typical American hustler bar crowd). Lots of cuties still for sale, most at $100 and more a pop, but for Rob Lowe look-alikes it might just be worth it. Drinks are extraordinarily expensive. A draft beer will run $3.25. But this East Side temple of decadence intends to keep the street trash out and their prices up—and we're not just talking about the drinks.

RUNYON'S

932 Second Avenue (between 49th and 50th Streets)

☎ **759-7801**

Named for Damon Runyon, the Bard of Broadway, this bar has moved from its original location around the corner after years of being one of Manhattan's most popular sports bars. Athletes, producers, announcers, and fans alike flood the place before, during, and after the big games. Multiple television sets offer relief for the "which game to watch" dilemma. Runyon's does a brisk after-work business as well, mostly for the over-thirty-five professional crowd who are delighted to drop their *Advertising Age* on the bar and talk to old friends or make new ones. The bar itself is a beauty: an elegant etched-glass mirror reflects the blond wood with its elephant-head brass bar rail. The restaurant in back and upstairs serves steaks, burgers, and seafood at moderate prices. If you're looking to find out the odds on tomorrow's big game, which athlete or even what stock is about to be traded, then this is the place for you.

RUPPERT'S
269 Columbus Avenue (between 72nd and 73rd Streets)
☎ 873-9400

If you decide to stroll up the avenue on a casual Sunday afternoon, then you might try a quick pick-me-up and a long sit-me-down at this centrally located spot. A relaxed, easygoing local crowd adds warmth and charm to this smoky, wood-paneled Columbus Avenue favorite. Come dressed in your favorite Shetland sweater and try a late Sunday-afternoon drink with the Sunday *Times*. Whether you are meeting friends or coming alone, the friendly fraternal feeling you get here is reminiscent of a college bar, where everyone knows everyone by sight, but not necessarily by name. But this one is a step better—you can be pretty certain that no one here will actually know you by name. What a relief. Leave your alumni T-shirt at home.

RUSTY'S
1271 Third Avenue (at 73rd Street)
☎ 861-4518

As you enter, a sign at the end of the bar reads NOT RE-SPONSIBLE FOR LOST CLOTHING, and makes you wonder exactly what goes on in here. In case you do lose your cloth-ing, though, they sell Rusty's jackets ($50), Mets 25th Anniversary Shirts ($35), sweatshirts, T-shirts, hats, vi-sors, and even books by and about the Mets. Not coinci-dentally, the owner is the former Mets right fielder and pinch hitter Rusty Staub, who's now an announcer and special assistant to the Mets' general manager. Rusty's is a hangout not only for the Mets, but for the Jets, the Giants, the Knicks, and visiting out-of-town teams. Accordingly, sports announcers, producers, and reporters flock here to interview the professionals and the fans. There is only one big-screen television, but every table in the main room is strategically situated. The best view is at the long tile bar, which has an indented elbow rest and is separated from the tables by a wooden partition. The floors are bare wood and the walls are completely covered with pictures of celebrities and sports stars. Rusty's does a booming business after work, at the dinner hour, and on weekends for brunch at game time. Rusty's gets stronger every year and is one of New York's favorite year-round sports bars.

SAFARI GRILL

1115 Third Avenue (between 65th and 66th Streets)

☎ 371-9090

This sleek and stately eatery adds another trendy architectural statement to the fashionable East Sixties. A bit out of place in this neck of the world, Safari feels more like a Tribeca spot, sporting a large and airy space, cool marble surfaces, mirrored walls, soft lighting, and safari-theme zebra-striped bar stools. Imagine a chic cocktail lounge in the Nairobi Marriott—even the waiters wear little kitschy safari shirts and matching bandannas. A large separate bar area occupies the front part of the restaurant and tends to get a crowd late at night. For such a pretty spot, it is surprising that Safari doesn't do a better after-work business. Nevertheless, Safari offers a sophisticated, quiet restaurant bar where one can go with a friend and enjoy privacy, comfort, and the chance to wear your latest Banana Republic wardrobe.

THE SAINT
105 Second Avenue (at 6th Street)
☎ **674-8369**

No book on bars would be complete without an ode to New York's Saint. For surely the Saint is not only a part of history for New Yorkers, but is probably one of the most well-known bars on the international circuit, particularly to the Fire Island–Mykonos trade. Housed in the original Fillmore East on Second Avenue, the Saint opened its doors in the late seventies and was designed as a playground for homosexual hedonism. Nothing came close to the Saint. Open only on weekends, it had the best dance floor, the best lights, the best drugs, the best sex. With its strict membership door policy, the Saint ensured itself of the legendary "A" crowd—young, incredibly good-looking, rich, and muscular. Yes, the all-American guppie crowd. Designers and fashion folk sported the latest in body waxes, tambourines, ethyl chloride, and jockstraps. The Saint's clientele would spend their week pumping up for an all-night blitz, then spend the rest of the week recuperating. This was homo heaven—thousands of bodies dancing to orgasmic heights under a light show that rivaled the planetarium. And when the boys got tired of dancing under the stars, a sojourn to the balcony turned up some of the hottest anonymous sex that money could buy. But dancing, drugs, sex, and scandal all came to a close when AIDS appeared on the horizon and men were forced to rethink their lifestyles. The balcony was closed and the late-night set started staying home to watch VCR porno and eat wheat germ. When the crowd started to die out (no pun intended), the club was financially endangered. Fear not: when homosexual money ebbed, heterosexual money was eagerly waiting in the wings. Special "straight" nights and charity events starring Dina Merrill began to pop up. The Saint became very chic for the very straight. What was once the secret of the young and the homo has now become a mainstream downtown disco catering to a young single secretary crowd, Staten Island and other assorted borough folk willing to pay a $15 cover for the chance to be cool. Bar drinks, served with free popcorn at the huge downstairs bar surrounded by carpeted tiered seating, are not only expensive, but something of a novelty for this after-hours juice bar now licensed for liquor. On a good night, hit a private party, have your admission waived, and go with friends. You can still enjoy the glorious dancing. Although the lighting effects have not changed and are still working their magic, if you look closely you can sense that something has changed; there is a certain haze over what was once a beautiful intensity.

ST. MORITZ HOTEL
50 Central Park South (at Sixth Avenue)
☎ 755-5800

CAFÉ DE LA PAIX For uptown sidewalk-cafe drinking, it's hard to beat Café de la Paix's prime location. Located in Central Park South's St. Moritz Hotel, Café de le Paix offers unobstructed views of Central Park and its environs. On a warm spring day, the views of Central Park West and Fifth Avenue are awesome; few dispute the beauty of this part of Manhattan. While the obvious draw here is a table on the outdoor wraparound terrace, the less popular indoor cocktail lounge also holds some surprises. Although fewer visitors seek out the gaudy interior lounge, few know about the gracious, elaborate, and tasty hors d'oeuvres served daily to its patrons. Fresh shrimp, assorted cheeses, crudité, and other treats are set out only for the crowd sitting inside. Be prepared to be faced with a major life decision: outside, the view, inside, the food. Let *your* insides be the judge. Neither choice will be disappointing.

ST. REGIS GRILL
2 East 55th Street (at Fifth Avenue)
☎ 753-4500

Located in the St. Regis–Sheraton Hotel, built by John Jacob Astor in 1907 to resemble a French château, the Grill offers a brightly lit lobby lounge where one can sit quietly and comfortably and order anything from tea to tequila. This outer room attracts lots of bouffant ladies all dressed in very proper attire sitting around in small clusters and conversing in dulcet tones; but inside you will discover a completely different atmosphere. The bar at the Grill offers a sophisticated, sleek, and elegant setting in a dark, dressy, romantic bar. Although there is a semicircular bar in the center of the room, most of the older, well-dressed patrons sit at individual tables. Men in expensive European designer suits have equally well-dressed mates. Although businessmen meet here to discuss the latest mergers, the dark and elegant feel of the room lends itself to romantic drinks, an intimate rendezvous, and close encounters of the best kind.

THE SALOON
1920 Broadway (at 64th Street)
☎ 874-1500

Large, loud, cavernous, attractive, and only a stone's throw away from Lincoln Center. Literally packed before and after curtain time, the Saloon caters to Upper West Side and Lincoln Center folk and features a menu as long as a Wagnerian opera offering just about everything from soup to nuts. The large and informal bar is a perfect rendezvous point for before-theater drinks. If you can't find a place to sit, the bar area has been designed with plenty of space to stand. When the weather starts to warm up, it's hard to find a better place for Upper West Side people-watching than this sidewalk cafe. A good standby. If the frenetics are simply too much, try its quieter mate, the Saloon Grill, just around the corner.

SAM'S CAFE
1406 Third Avenue (at 80th Street)
☎ 988-5300

Blue neon lettering against a large picture window adds an appropriate Hollywood touch to this trendy East Side eatery. Named for proprietor and creator Mariel "Sam" Hemingway, Sam's Cafe stands out as something of a star in and of itself on the upper–Third Avenue strip. Aesthetically pleasing to the eye, the room is inviting, comfortable, airy, and terrifically lit. A large poster of a cow hung in the center of the bar, rodeo-style bar stools, light wood paneling, and wooden floors define the casual country feel of this space. We are not talking country French— we're talking Georgia O'Keeffe country. The bar itself is long and inviting, runs the length of the restaurant, and attracts a lively after-work clientele. Most come with dates or friends and stay pretty much to themselves. A relaxed, clean-lined, down-home feeling adds a refreshing touch to what could easily be a snooty Upper East Side Hollywood bistro. My hunch is that we can thank "Sam's" personality for keeping that in line.

SAM'S RESTAURANT
152 West 52nd Street (between Sixth and Seventh Avenues)
☎ 582-8700

One assumes that the addition of the office space created by the recently completed Equitable Center will produce hardworking, expense-account money in pursuit of new gastronomic delights. Witness the rapid growth of this neighborhood and the assumption is obviously proved correct. Within a one-block radius one can dine in a few of New York's most stellar spots: Palio, Le Bernandin, Bellini, and now the latest arrival on the block, Sam's Restaurant. Clearly the shirt-sleeve counterpart to its more formal neighbors, Sam's is owned by the same celebrity Hemingway-Crissman clan who opened the popular Sam's Cafe on the Upper East Side. However, straying from their success as small bistro owners, the duo decided to open a larger scaled, moderately priced midtown eatery that could take advantage of a busy lunchtime trade while remaining trendy and continuing to court their Hollywood crowd. But for some reason, even though a great deal of time, money, and effort was obviously spent decorating its twenty-eight-foot high-ceilinged space, the room just doesn't work. Brown wood tables with matching captain's chairs, western accessories, and a mural by James Rosenquist are supposed to give the room a country flavor. But take the Hollywood pizazz out from Mariel's name and you are left with a room no more exciting than a banquet room at a Holiday Inn. Just looking at the brown patterned carpet makes you think "Steak & Ale." However, a large, wooden, circular bar is separated from the restaurant and fits quietly into one end of the room, which offers the opportunity to observe the restaurant without having to participate. Although the majority of clients are awaiting tables in the restaurant, the size, design, and location of the bar make it an attractive rendezvous point to meet friends after work for a quick drink before the theater. Overlook the room's decor and go for a quick drink-and-go; then giddyap up-town to Sam's Cafe for a more palatable experience.

SARDI'S

234 West 44th Street (between Broadway and Eighth Avenue)
☎ 221-8440

If Broadway has a star of a bar, it certainly must be Sardi's. After all, where else does one go on opening night to wait for one's reviews? How many film classics have been shot in Sardi's sanctum to give us, the public, an insider's peek into backstage life? I'm sorry to report that the legendary bar and restaurant at Sardi's is soon to become part of history. Sold by its owner, George Sardi, infamous in his own right, Sardi's will be rolling up its red carpet in the not too distant future. So, if you haven't been to Sardi's yet—don't walk, run, and drink in this legendary institution. The small, intimate bar to the left of the stately entranceway is ideal for a drink either before or after curtain. Centrally located to all of the theaters, Sardi's offers its patrons a sense of theatrical elegance, formality, and tradition. The dress is conservative and proper; a navy blazer is perfect. The restaurant's main draw is the downstairs dining room. Red checkered tablecloths and legendary caricatures of the very famous clientele abound. Upstairs is reserved for out-of-town diners and movie star searchers. Sardi's has been and continues to be *the* place for theater folk; particularly after opening nights and other assorted invitational theater galas. Drinks are pricey—but go, for how many nights do you get the chance to see Liz chomping on a mushroom cheeseburger? 'Swonderful.

SAVAGE

208 West 23rd Street (between 7th and 8th Avenues)

☎ **691-4421**

The decor is retro seventies. The feel is definitely eighties. Even when the mercury drops to thirty below zero, it's still hot in here. Nothing seems to stop the endless throngs of anxious patrons fresh onto the scent of a new club. Probably a flash in the pan and closed by publication of this book, this mirrored vintage disco hall caters to a black audience every night of the week except for Tuesday. But if it's Tuesday, it must be Savage; the latest trendy spot where the downtown set gets decadent. Red banquettes, chrome and glass cocktail tables, mirrored walls, and spinning disco ball bring back memories of Donna Summer and Studio 54 days. The crowd is young and trendy, but the conspicuous absence of adults is disappointing. Tama Janowitz look-alikes and Oriental designers push through bumper-to-bumper crowds. Everyone seems to be dressed in black. Music is loud funk and boogie. An elevated oval dance floor dominates the center of the room. By midnight the place is uncomfortably crowded and lines snake from the coatroom upstairs into the lobby. A total bore. By 12:30, too many folks have been let in and the room becomes dangerously crowded, having filled up with a more mainstream crowd. The really hot crowd that arrived earlier has moved on. Orchestrate an early entrance and easy escape or plan on picking up your coat the following morning. Oh, and by the way, this club is so hot simply from word of mouth, never admit to having read about it here. So hot, we'll see how long it lasts.

SHELTER
540 Second Avenue (at 30th Street)
☎ 684-4207

Globe lamps on wooden poles are reflected in the long mirror above the bar. They look like streetlights, but they're only lighting the booths directly behind the bar. There are discreet track lights above the bar, and a television at each end. The picture windows could be framing views of Indianapolis or Idaho, for all we know. The atmosphere feels generic, but in an inoffensive, almost comforting way. Kind of like eating at McDonald's when you're in a foreign country.

SHOUT
124 West 43rd Street (between Broadway and Sixth Avenue)
☎ 869-2088

If it's been too long since you've heard "Wooly Bully" or "Land of 1000 Dances," then it's time you made a pilgrimage to Shout and reveled in the most danceable music in America. The best go-go dancers this side of *Shindig* take turns on the stage and sometimes lead the crowd through dances like the locomotion (where they hook up like a train and make tracks all over the club) or Simon Sez, or even the Addams Family. And that's not to mention the roller-skaters or the giant video screen that sometimes drops down behind the dance floor. Once the Henry Miller Theater, Shout is still quite theatrical. The backstage area is painted black and doubles as an elevated dance floor and stage. A 1950s car has crashed through the back wall and stays suspended there in midair. There's a replica of a huge Victrola, but the speaker is now a video screen that features programs like *The Flintstones*. The walls are all black, but the columns and ornate moldings

177

are painted glossy red. The male employees wear white letter sweaters with a red *S* and the girls wear white blouses with short red flared skirts—they look like carhops. The DJ is stationed in what used to be the box seats and around those boxes on both sides of the club are gigantic neon arches. The balcony has been converted to a VIP lounge where a $20 admission fee entitles you to escape to the rafters for a breath of fresh air. The seats have been replaced with car seats (complete with headrests) and are separated by drive-in movie speakers. A refurbished Wurlitzer glows brightly and a Harley Davidson à la *Easy Rider* sits in front of an American flag. There are cocktail tables set up along the rail of the balcony and to the side and back of the dance floor. The large bar to the back of the dance floor is set off by a glass brick wall that is lighted from inside with pastel colors. A mural of 1950s-style cars at a drive-in movie brightens the area behind the bar. A second bar set up like a candy counter is located in the front, so you never have to leave the dance floor. How civilized! The coatcheck and restrooms are located downstairs along a spacious pink and gray corridor. There's also a shop that sells wonderful kitsch items like Etch-A-Sketch, Mr. Potato Head, Pez, Gumby, Hoola-Hoops, postcards, and Shout T-shirts. There's live music on Wednesday nights; such sixties stars as Lou Christie and Tommy James and the Shondells have appeared. They don't advertise, but you can be put on their mailing list. Regular admission is $10, but Wednesday through Friday admission is $5 from five P.M. 'til eight P.M. and includes one free drink plus a buffet. The crowd is young and old, black and white, hip and square, and the employees are enthusiastic and courteous. Shout was put together with careful attention to details, and is obviously run with love and care.

SIBERIA

804 Washington Street (between Horatio and Gansevoort Streets)

☎ **463-8521**

If the Russians *are* coming and have decided to launch their very own club, then one cannot help but wonder why they have chosen this spot. If we have been led to believe that Siberia is about wide-open spaces and existing far away and apart from everything else, then one has difficulty understanding how this claustrophobic spot smack in the middle of West Village condo haven has gotten its name. There seems to be an innate contradiction in terms. Siberia has recently opened its doors and is billing itself as a downtown performance space; its ability to promote itself and maintain a lively crowd remains to be proven. After having been decreed acceptable by the doorman for admittance, one pushes open heavy glass doors and is hit with an immediate sense of harshness. Obviously pretty is "out," and steely is "in." Feeling a bit like an after-hours Parisian joint, this linoleum-floored, multilevel space, outfitted with a myriad of black industrial stairways, is marred by lack of elbow room—so it's built up rather than out. Staircases lead to two tiny adjacent lounges having the look and feel of typical VIP club lounges. Contrary to the usual policy in Russia and in New York club life, where all people are not created equal, the lounges here are, surprisingly, open for the general public to enjoy the view of the club below. The crowd here, although it has yet to settle down into anything distinguishable, seems to be sprinkled with the downtown vanguard set. The small bar is scaled in proportion to the rest of the room and offers seating for twelve. Taking its very first baby steps, Siberia might take a while to warm up.

SIGN OF THE DOVE
1110 Third Avenue (at 65th Street)
☎ **861-8080**

Prime Upper East Side sedate chic, where the limos park
for expense-account dinners. Still offers a pretty, romantic, elegant spot for quiet drinks. Dove remains a good
standby, albeit pricey, for a quiet recuperative after a spree
through Bloomies or for an elegant nightcap after the theater. A well-heeled and sophisticated crowd practically demands proper attire. Wear your most traditional blue blazer,
and don't forget to pack your most stylish billfold; you'll
need it.

SILVERBIRDS
505 Columbus Avenue (near 84th Street)
☎ **877-7777**

Billed as the first American Indian restaurant in New
York, this new addition to Columbus Avenue looks like
something out of Disneyland. Strategically placed oversized cactus plants and wonderful Navajo carpets frame
the free-form bar, which opens onto a very popular sidewalk cafe. If you could imagine an Indian reservation
somewhere in Cheyenne that would serve dinner and drinks
(without requiring a reservation), you've got the feel of
Silverbirds. The menu is focused on American Indian
cuisine and, as one would expect, its crowd reflects this
focus. You will see lots of full-blooded Indian folk eating and drinking and looking quite at home. When you
visit the bar and see the crowd you can't help but wonder *why* this has not been done before in this Manhattan
melting pot. Or then again, perhaps the questions should
be *how*?

SMITH & WOLLENSKY
201 East 49th Street (at Third Avenue)
☎ 753-1530

An extremely pretty and gracious bar shares the grounds of this very popular and recently refurbished Third Avenue steak restaurant. A large square-shaped room with plenty of bar stools and comfortable tables adds to the warm and convivial atmosphere; the copper-topped bar, wooden floors, and wonderful architectural details add to the charm and "specialness." The bar gets busy after work with advertising and Third Avenue folk, three-piece suits, and expense-account diners. Many use the bar as a rendezvous point; the sheer size and physical beauty of the bar attracts many diners to have their first cocktail at the bar rather than being seated immediately. Elegant and understated, the bar at Smith & Wollensky is well worth your while for midtown drinking. Check out the corner clock. When you see the big hand on the twelve, and the little hand on the six, you can count on a crowd beginning to stream in.

B. SMITH'S
771 Eighth Avenue (at 47th Street)
☎ 247-2222

All of a sudden, in the midst of Hell's Kitchen, up the street from the Hollywood Twin theater, comes the latest in Eighth Avenue gentrification. B. Smith's opened its swank new doors, adding an architectural stunner to the neighborhood. A sleek glass-and-cement corner facade immediately draws your eye to the striking interior. The large bar area, separate from the restaurant, is a clean white airy space with high white ceilings, dark gray floors, and a shiny silver high-tech bar beneath two fabulous pyramidlike skylights. The look is loftlike slick with a Tribeca feel. The bar seats twenty-five but is built with an expansive standing area to accommodate a much larger crowd. The crowd tends to be upscale, young sophisticates dressed in cool business attire—well dressed, well groomed, well financed—and seems to be attracting a large black clientele. If you get bored with the crowd inside, then the floor-to-ceiling picture windows lining the perimeter of the room offer additional street options. Interesting, exciting, lively, and appropriately theatrical for the neighborhood. Ideal for before- or after-theater drinks. With a little publicity, this place will undoubtedly take off.

SMOKE STACKS LIGHTNING
380 Canal Street (at West Broadway)
☎ 226-0485

This corner bar on the boundary of Soho, Tribeca, and Chinatown has become something of a chameleon. Depending on the time of day, and day of the week, you might very well find a completely different crowd. It is indeed the crowd at Smoke Stacks that makes for its most distinctive feature. Businessmen from the neighborhood pour themselves in during lunch; and at night, a slow trickle of neighborhood folk meet after work for quiet drinks. But the most interesting quirk here is on weekend nights. On a typical Saturday night, Smoke Stacks Lightning is filled with lots of young, well-dressed Chinese, and functions as a neighborhood bar for this community. So don't be surprised if you walk into the room and feel like you took a wrong turn in Chinatown. Relax: it may very well be the flavor you have wanted to taste. Otherwise, the place itself is pretty Tribeca normal—exposed brick walls and gray columns, black ceilings, video monitors, and large floor-to-ceiling windows give the room a cool feel. Leafy plants serve as punctuation to the picture. A well-designed zig-zag bar with angled overhead mirrors makes it easy to scout everyone in the house in one fell swoop. But if you want to catch up on gossip with an old friend, grab a booth in the early evening and chat away. You will find it comfortable and private. Add television, video games, and a jukebox and you have all the necessary distractions. So, if the crowd after work is on the "Column A" side, and weekend nights on "Column B", then you may very well want to try a night from "Column A," and come back to try "Column B."

S.O.B.'s

204 Varick Street (at Houston Street)

☎ **243-4940**

Imagine an update of Ricky Ricardo's Tropicana nightclub and you have the concept—elevated bandstand center stage, rectangular dance floor set at its feet, and long narrow tables surrounding the dance floor. Mix Ricky's Cuban "Babalu" with salsa, Caribbean funk, and reggae drawn from an international palette of Latin, African, and Caribbean tunes, and you've got the beat. Replace an Ethel Mertz white-bread audience with a comfortable mixture of Brazilians, Haitians, yuppies, punks, and Wall Streeters. Hang gourds from the ceiling, line the walls with snakeskins, vibrant Haitian art, and drums, and you know Ricky and his Tropicana Lounge have been left far behind. A one-time coffee shop, the Sounds of Brazil, opened in 1982, has managed to continue to attract and delight a steady clientele undeterred by its hefty $15 admit fee. Judging from the size of the crowd, whether it be weekend or weeknight, you can tell that S.O.B.'s is not exactly hurting for patronage. Yes, they certainly are doing something right. Call ahead and check on the group scheduled to perform later in the evening. Depending upon the group's following, S.O.B.'s can be mobbed midweek. If you want a table, it's best to call for reservations. No reservations are required to enjoy the large bar area, however, which generally starts to get going at around eleven P.M. There isn't much bar seating, but you will find yourself on your feet anyway, rocking to the beat of the music, perhaps even propelled to the dance floor. S.O.B.'s bar is relaxed, dark, and comfortably sleazy; the bar menu offers enough delights to transport you to faraway islands in no time flat. Try a Caipirinha, the Brazilian national drink, composed of sugar-cane liquor, sugar, and freshly crushed lime, and watch your body start talking. Look around—everybody is moving some part of their body. Infectiously festive, relaxed, and lively, lacking in attitude and pretension, S.O.B.'s continues to offer a tropical escape in an exotic and uninhibiting atmosphere.

SOFI
102 Fifth Avenue (near 15th Street)
☎ 463-8888

A new geographic district, South of the Flatiron district, now boasts its very own acronym—SOFI. And "Sofi's Choice" restaurant is clearly Sofi, a strikingly romantic new establishment. Opened this year by Richard Lavin, owner of Lavin's on West 39th Street, Sofi occupies the soaring loft space formerly occupied by Fifth Avenue Grill, now completely redesigned. The new room is a knockout: elegant, formal, and sophisticated. One cannot help but be impressed by its beauty. A small foyer, reminiscent of a lobby in a European hotel, contains comfortable upholstered chairs and couches conducive to sipping intimate aperitifs while sizing up the crowd. Swing around and enjoy a Fifth Avenue view. Take a step down and enter the dining room, a long cavernous room with a rim of tables tucked away in a second-story loft. Sconces shooting light up along the burnt sienna walls adorned with paintings, tapestries, and brightly woven oriental rugs complete the visual delight.

The handsome dark wooden bar is equally impressive. It boasts thirteen stools and black-rimmed reading lamps, and offers an extensive list of wines to sample by the glass. Although Sofi's bar crowd is drawn primarily from its dressy restaurant clientele, one should not miss a room this special. Ideal for a quiet celebration. Best for a "Midnight Love Affair."

THE SOHO KITCHEN AND BAR
130 Greene Street (between Spring and Prince Streets)
☎ 925-1866

The one-year-old Soho Kitchen and Bar is owned by the Greene Street people, and is an oenophile's paradise. A large wraparound bar with exposed beams and many small comfortable tables offers an ideal setting to enjoy the luxury of tasting any of 125 wines sold by the glass from what is said to be the largest cruvinet system in the world. For a true vineyard adventurer, the bar offers special "flight tastings" from every category on its list. A flight tasting allows patrons to sample as many as eight varieties of a particular kind of wine, such as chardonnay or sauvignon blanc; the Soho Kitchen offers eleven possible flight tastings, served in 1½-ounce glasses. Comfortable, laid-back, and not particularly popular or crowded, the Kitchen offers a chance to learn about wines in a very Soho setting and walk away with a very pleasant buzz.

SOUTHERN FUNK CAFE

330 West 42nd Street (between Eighth and Ninth Avenues)

☎ **564-6560**

The old McGraw-Hill building, that art deco jukebox with alternating bands of windows and blue-green terra-cotta tiles, just ain't what it used to be since those gauzy pink, white trash curtains went up in the front windows. Not to mention the neon beer signs hanging in the windows and inside on the screaming pink, green, and gold walls. Gloriously high tack! This is the perfect pit stop if you have time to fill before dropping into a play on Theatre Row or into the depths of the dread Port Authority. The crowd here reflects the offbeat, eclectic mixture of folk who happen to know the place's whereabouts. A shark hovers above the 42nd Street exit, a life-size inflated alligator hangs from midceiling, and posters of crawfish dot the walls. The menu is a delight for misplaced Southerners, with treats like chicken and dumplings, fried okra, hush puppies, and yo' mamma's apple pie. The homey feeling is enhanced by padded chrome and vinyl kitchen chairs, which share the floor with soda-shop booths. A long soda counter, loaded with goodies and Mardi Gras beads, is backed by a black tile wall; the remaining walls and interior columns boast the original black and green art deco tilework. Rockabilly, R&B, and early rock 'n' roll provide the nonstop backbeat for the bustling employees, who still manage to be laid-back and friendly. True to their word, they put the "fun" in funk.

SOUTH STREET SEAPORT
Water and Fulton Streets
☎ 732-7678

A welcome addition to the downtown area, the South Street
Seaport boasts hundreds of places to snack, shop, browse,
see, taste, and feel. It's as close to a sensory overload as
one can get in New York. There is something for everyone,
from out-of-towners to jaded New Yorkers. One should
stop by to take in this delightful scene—even if it's just to
accommodate your visiting Aunt Tillie from Tucson. You
can always decide to ditch Tillie and seek refuge in one of
the many watering holes. If you do, you will have absolutely no problem finding a place. Let your feet and your
mood wander and take you where you want to be. Beware
of Friday afternoons. Yuppies and preppies in suits and
running shoes from uptown and downtown converge on
the seaport as if the city were in the midst of an evacuation
and Battery Park was decreed the first point of embar-
kation.

At the very end of the dock you will find the popular
Flutie's, a two-level corner bar and restaurant offering
unobstructed views of the East River and Brooklyn Heights
with enough singles looking to meet other eligibles to even
make Yenta the Matchmaker blush. If you're so inclined,
by all means give it a shot. Other standbys worth inves-
tigating are Roeblings, the Fulton Street Cafe, McDuffy's
Irish Coffee House, the Liberty Cafe, Gianni's, Sgarlato's,
Pedro O'Hare's, Sloppy Lou's, Sweets, and Caroline's
Comedy Club. Thursday nights are particularly busy at the
North Star Pub when sailing teams from Goldman Sachs,
Prudential-Bache, and other investment houses wind up
here to drink and watch videos of their races earlier that
evening. You might try and wander over to the new Ocean
Reefe Grille, a magnificent and overscaled delight that
comes as close to Disneyland as one gets east of the Mis-
sissippi. Thirteen museum-quality boats suspended from

187

the rafters by steel cables silhouetted against a midnight sky provide dramatic focus for this show-stopper restaurant.

Take a walk around the seaport—South Street has something for everyone. A sure crowd-pleaser; row your boat gently down the stream and dock for a drink. Life may just become a dream.

SPARKS

210 East 46th Street (between Second and Third Avenues)
☎ 687-4855

Home of Mafia slayings, power steaks, and pricey dinners, Sparks offers a rather small side bar used predominantly by diners awaiting tardy arrivals. I recommend the bar at Sparks for two purposes:

1. If you are in the East 40s and are pressed for a quiet and remote pubby spot to conduct man-to-man business over a bottle of wine and can use the smell of filet mignon in the background to close the deal, by all means go.

2. When a curious relative from out of town shows up and wants to go to a famous New York City restaurant where "real" Mafia people eat, by all means go. If they are really good (or bad), you can take them outside to scout bloodstains on the sidewalk. Always good for a cheap thrill.

SPORTING CLUB

99 Hudson Street (between Franklin and Harrison Streets)
☎ 219-0900

Budding young Wall Streeters on their way home from work, white button-down collars, yellow ties, and a Michelob crowd add to the loud, lively, and fraternal feeling at this clever Tribeca hot spot. Imagine what the decor of a club for sports enthusiasts would be like—clubby, masculine, smoky, with red walls and lots of video monitors—and you get the picture. Wherever you are, wherever you look, squeezed in between all the wonderful sports photographs and memorabilia on the walls, you will be in clear sight of one of the many video screens. The largest screen, and the focus of the club, is mounted front and center over the large square-shaped bar. Not only do you get a bird's-eye view of the sporting event of the evening, but off to the side you can view a running scoreboard of other major sporting events taking place simultaneously.

Although the concept behind this club is extremely clever, the crowd tends to be a little less than clever. Even though you will find limos parked outside, the crowd is predominantly young, straight, very preppie, and very segregated. The sweater girls stand together, while the men guzzle beers and shout at the screen. If you go with friends, you can stand at the bar or choose from one of the many tables around the room, including a spot up on the balcony. Gimmicky tablecloths with imprinted scorecards and a stash of crayons add a clever touch. If you really are a sports buff, and enjoy the camaraderie of other sports enthusiasts, then this rowdy little spot might very well prove to be a home run of an evening for you.

STRINGFELLOWS
35 East 21st Street (between Park Avenue South and Broadway)
☎ 254-2444

Black stretch limousines glide up to smoked glass doors and deliver patrons into the hands of three doormen who ensure a safe and easy arrival. After clearing "Customs" and a $25 admit fee, you enter the large front bar and restaurant reminiscent of a sophisticated European club. Mirrors, black walls, black ceilings, pink leather chairs, and potted palms give a sense of swank and formality. The raised dining room has been designed to offer patrons a view of the bar as well as to afford privacy by adding etched-glass partitions. Patrons dine on expensive prix-fixe dinners and order exotic drinks in the $25 price range. Some order champagne at $350 a bottle, while others indulge in the world's most expensive Dom Perignon cocktail at $500 a throw. Yes, we're talking big bucks here. Diamond rings, sequined tops, mink collars, designer party dresses, and Armani suits mingle in an air pungent with Giorgio and Poison. At about eleven P.M., mirrored doors open to reveal the discotheque. The ladies and gentlemen in attendance filter into the moderate-size black dance room with designer neon lights and a dance floor reminiscent of *Saturday Night Fever*. Two smaller bars and a specially roped-off section for patrons desiring champagne complete the room. Decadent, yes. Festive, yes. Dull, rarely. International bankers, gold traders, filmmakers, and jewelry designers dance designer shoes away until the wee hours of the morning. Major old-time money on the way home from a benefit at the Met have drivers wait outside while they nightcap and share the floor with a predominantly mid-thirties crowd attractive and dressed to the hilt. Club members pay $500 a year in dues or can opt for a $5,000-a-year gold card. Elegant, dressy, and formal, Stringfellow's is undoubtedly the Nancy Reagan filter-down effect to club life in the eighties. A slice of New York that can be fun for the right mood and a healthy pocketbook.

SUNSET STRIP

95 Horatio Street (at Bethune Street)

☎ 645-0808

Absolutely trendy and up to the very minute, this West Village eatery is a must for the trite and trendy crowd. Handpainted psychedelic and zebra-striped furniture and bar, punk waiters, and a hot Tribeca crowd make this place cook. The restaurant is designed to take advantage of the fabulous unobstructed view of the Hudson River. You can sip cocktails and watch Malcom Forbes's yacht cruise by. The cruising indoors is not bad either. A long counter facing the river is set up in the bar area, enabling singles to dine alone without feeling stigmatized. It's wonderful to arrive in time to see the sun set over Hoboken—don't worry about venturing out at this ungodly and unchic hour, for this is the ideal time to check out this bar. The crowd is attractive, interesting, and loud, and offers some good possibilities. Go with friends and perhaps leave with new ones. This Strip is hot.

THE SURF CLUB

415 East 91st Street (between York and First Avenues)

☎ 410-1360

The crowd behind the cordon is restless and resentful; these people are used to being waited on, not waiting in line. Upstairs, the middle section of the main room is cordoned off and filled with tables, many of which wear RESERVED signs. The poolside-style tables are even complete with umbrellas. The long bar has mirrors behind it with blue shutters on either side. Giant sharks and blue marlins hang on the wall and surfboards hang from the ceiling. A silver disco ball hangs over the dance floor and shoots sparks of light over the hardwood floor. They even play some disco music here, along with older songs by the likes of David Bowie and the Jackson Five. The people are packed in like sardines here, but the atmosphere is more like a country club or a yacht club than a surf club. Most of the men wear suits and ties and the women are dressed like it's New Year's Eve: velvet, taffeta, low-cut evening dresses with long, full skirts, bows on almost every head of hair, and of course the requisite pearls dripping from every available appendage. The crowd is mostly in their twenties and thirties, but there are a few forty-, fifty-, and even sixty-year-olds floating about. One handsome young man confided in hushed tones that he was very, very rich and that he only came here to get laid. Indeed, this place lends a whole new meaning to the term *debutante ball*. It's just like the Beach Boys say: "She'll have fun, fun, fun till her Daddy takes the T-Bird away." The upper crust of a very well bred, white-bread society.

TAPIS ROUGE

157 Duane Street (between Hudson Street and West Broadway)
☎ 732-5555

Ever since it received a two-star rating in the *New York Times*, this Tribeca room has been booked. Priding themselves on quality French bistro fare, the charming owners, Jean Goutal and Toni Bodini, have created an equally appealing interior. Black fluted chairs and crisp white tablecloths complement the Fred-and-Ginger black-and-white tiled floor. The small wooden bar tucked away in the front corner of the restaurant has been carefully restored and functions primarily as a space for diners awaiting tables. However, Tapis Rouge offers an intimate, pretty Tribeca bar well suited for nightcaps. Considering the location of this restaurant, the crowd seems a bit misplaced. Upper East Siders, jackets and ties, and designer dresses make their way downtown to enjoy dining with the downtown set. Too bad they only look at one another. Don't think of coming alone—bring a friend and force an intimate conversation. Meet Jean, he'll easily dispel the myth of French unfriendliness.

TASTINGS
144 West 55th Street (between Sixth and Seventh Avenues)
☎ 757-1160

Midtown lunch and expense-account chic, across the street from City Center, Tastings is one of the older wine bars in town. The International Wine Center, one of the major wine schools in the city, operates in quarters atop the restaurant, and offers a relaxing bar with twenty-five choices of wines to sample by the glass. There's a fine selection even for the most discriminating wine palate—one can choose various vintages at various prices, with a top vintage demanding as much as $20 a glass. The earthy and simple decor, somewhat loud and animated, makes this establishment ideal for "playing" in foreign vineyards. Any wine-tasting bar, especially one this popular, is by nature pretty friendly. You might even get to taste your neighbor's vintage—and in case you've forgotten, we're talking about wine. Great for a lunchtime buzz or an after-work chaser. If you try both, I promise not to tell.

TAVERN ON THE GREEN
Central Park at 67th Street
☎ 873-3200

Forget all the tacky Folger coffee commercials shot here, and make sure to stop by this landmark Central Park restaurant for drinks. Pay no attention to the tourists traveling with cameras and the blue-haired lady set, and save Tavern on the Green for a mild spring delight. Aside from Tavern on the Green's very beautiful Crystal Room, the outdoor brick patio cafe is an unexpected treat. Festive twinkling lights and pretty umbrella-topped tables combine to make the perfect setting for romantic and civilized drinks. The crowd is a good mixture of upscale sophisticates in suits and dresses and typical out-of-towners as well. If you happen to be "strolling in the park one day," particularly "in the merry, merry month of May," make sure you follow the yellow brick road into this wonderful Central Park retreat.

1018

515 West 18th Street (near Eleventh Avenue)

☎ 645-5156

Any establishment announcing the start of a party at exactly 10:18 P.M. sounds like my kind of place. Lodged in the former Roxy, 1018 has abandoned the concept of heels-on-wheels for a decidedly high-tech Chelsea dance spot. Fake cinderblock walls and requisite carpeted platforms create an industrial warehouse feel. Nothing new, nothing special, nothing particularly thematic. But if you do like to dance and enjoy plenty of space, then this cavernous room, boasting a very large dance floor, may be just your cup of tea. Unfortunately, the space can be far too large and overpowering for the number of bodies in attendance. And for this place to cook, the room has to be packed. Those that have managed to shake down the scene congregate around a pencil-thin oval bar. But the gem here is a glass-enclosed upstairs lounge which affords the viewer a bird's-eye view of the club in sensual, comfortable, and quiet surroundings. Although it is still too new to pass judgment, my gut reaction is that 1018 is simply too large to be special enough to attract a hip Manhattan patronage. But if you want to check it out, 1018, contrary to the invite, really starts to cook more at 12:18—and that's A.M.

THE TERRACE

400 West 119th Street (in Butler Hall; near Morningside Drive)
☎ 666-9490

Columbia University's attempted answer to Windows on the World. Atop the tenth floor of Butler Hall (Columbia housing for the legal eagle crowd) rests the renowned Terrace restaurant which has garnered critical acclaim for its spectacular views and gourmet dining. Unfortunately, both accolades elude me. The nondescript bar, located right off the elevator, offers a fine view of the downtown skyline, but its light wood, mirrored decor, and touristy ambience have the feel of a bar atop a Hyatt or Marriott hotel in San Francisco. If you are expecting an Ivy League feel with dark walls, rich wood, and leather sofas—forget it. And the crowd here seems to match the decor—uninteresting and uninspiring: lots of professors with visiting families in town for their annual "special-occasion" dinners. The bar, although surprisingly large in scale, is basically host to diners awaiting tables. If you must, stop by for a quick drink to take in the view. Don't even think of staying on for a candlelight dinner. The food is surprisingly expensive, boring and *très ordinaire*. If you're going to make the trek up to Columbia for drinks, keep on going and hit some of the more colorful clubs in Harlem. This spot ain't worth the trek nor the bucks.

TERRANOVA CAFE

18 West 38th Street (between Fifth and Sixth Avenues)
☎ 391-2123

An oasis in a desert of shops, stores, and office buildings. High ceilings, wooden floors, brick walls, lots of light and space and hanging plants . . . a pleasant throwback to the seventies. The music runs toward Dan Fogelberg or Jackson Browne, with live music nightly. This is a comfortable place to come for a late-afternoon beer or after shopping at B. Altman or Lord & Taylor. Incongruously, there are posters of attractive, scantily clad women, pin-ups masquerading as muscle pix, hanging around everywhere. Although the restaurant seems like an Amy's with a liquor license, the bar could be a lifesaver if you find yourself in this neighborhood on a cold winter night.

TOP OF THE SIXES
666 Fifth Avenue (at 52nd Street)
☎ 757-6662

Any bar atop thirty-nine floors overlooking Fifth Avenue and Central Park is not a sight one should easily miss in New York. And when the sun goes down and the city begins to light up, Top of the Sixes offers great potential as a "view bar." But you must keep in mind that the view to savor here is strictly out the panoramic windows overlooking Fifth Avenue and its environs. The light wood bar, tacky mirrored murals, and red upholstered swivel chairs do not exactly add panache. Until your eyes adjust to the lighting, the candlelit tables, brass trimmings, and baby grand piano look real attractive. Not catering to a particularly chic or elegant crowd, Sixes' large rectangular bar is extremely popular after work with middle-management folk, secretaries, young CPAs, and lots of out-of-towners, young and old alike. It's just a shame that this Stoufferrun restaurant has not tried any harder to freshen the place up. At the very least, they should rip out the stained carpeting. This place is acceptable for informal drinks with an out-of-town guest, but you can certainly do much better.

TOP OF THE TOWER

4 Mitchell Place (First Avenue and 49th Street)

☎ 355-7300

You're advised that proper attire is requested as you get on the express elevator to the twenty-sixth floor of the Beekman Tower Hotel. The hotel was opened in 1928 as the Panhellenic Hotel for women, and the Top of the Tower was a private officers' club during World War II. Today you're likely to find yourself sitting beside a Sutton Place matron or a delegate to the United Nations. The Top of the Tower retains the elegance and grace of an age gone by, and boasts original arched, eighteen-foot leaded-glass windows of art nouveau design. Tiny white lights sparkle on the potted ficus trees and ring the outer balcony. Even the black-and-white tiled bathroom is charming with its black sink and European attendant ever-ready with the liquid soap. Sit on the west side of the terrace to watch the sun set behind Citicorp and the Empire State Building. Then move to the east side where you can see the elevated subway weave its way into the heart of Queens, the red neon signs of Pepsi-Cola and Silvercup Studios, and the 59th Street Bridge. Simple hors d'oeuvres are offered Monday through Friday; Tuesday through Saturday there's live piano music; and there are often private parties on Sunday, so call ahead. A two-drink minimum is in effect from nine P.M. to one A.M.. The drinks are pricey, but this is the perfect place for a nightcap before heading home to slip into a silk nightgown. Very romantic, very New York.

TORTILLA FLATS
767 Washington Street (at Bethune Street)
☎ 243-1053

This animated corner Tex-Mex joint comfortably holds forty bodies and easily clears one hundred jumps with a young, preppie crowd. The decor is quasi–East Village—plain wooden tables, nondescript bar, 1950s tiled floor, low tacky ceilings, and blue and pink neon lighting fixtures. Bright twinkling lights that announce the Christmas season decorate white skeleton heads left over from Halloween. The music is so loud that if there was any more space, you would swear everyone would automatically start to dance. Young preppie types out for a "groovy" night on the town shape the partying and fraternal spirit here. Attire ranges from blue jeans to jackets and ties; the crowd pours in for beer drinking, loud music, and good-natured camaraderie. If you're lucky, you'll get a table; otherwise, squeeze yourself standing into this rockin' West Village scene.

TUBA CITY TRUCK STOP
1700 Second Avenue (at 88th Street)*
☎ 996-6200

Pull up to the bar and give yourself a boost with a Hydraulic Lift (a shot of gold tequila with a Dos Equis chaser), a Tuba City Turnpiker (a turquoise margarita) or a Grease-monkey (daily frozen specials). Tin signs advertising the likes of Squirt soda and Donald Duck bread adorn the walls, and license plates from various states hang on the back wall beside a real stoplight. Across the narrow cor-

---

*There's a West Side Tuba City at 2180 Broadway (at 77th Street), 362-4360.

ridor is a trompe l'oeil painting of an eighteen-wheeler driving through a Southwestern landscape of cacti and snowcapped mountains. The driver smirks, a real rebel flag behind his head. The white paper place mats are graced with a single black tire tread, and the motto on the back of the menu is "Where the elite eat to meet." The back dining room is a lively spot and is much requested by the younger folks, many of whom greet the waitresses by name. The staff is a curious mixture of uptown girls in pearls and downtown types whose shirts bear names like Thelma and Betty Lou. The crowd is youngish (twenties and thirties), but not the ultrahip trendmongers you'd expect to find in such a design-conscious environment. The owners have utilized the name-brand craze to blow their own horn a little and offer free Tuba City postcards at the bar. Very smart. The place fills up early and stays packed until the wee hours. The light is soft, the music's loud. Don't come here unless you want to have F-U-N.

TUNNEL

220 Twelfth Avenue (at 27th Street)

☎ **529-6324**

If you can manage to get past the doormen guarding the roped-off entrance (and the attitude that goes along with it), you enter this latest foray into disco club life. Spend thirty minutes waiting to have your coat checked by three women when there really should be ten, and you will be sufficiently charged to hit the dance floor. Spend ten minutes more walking through the huge space checking out the never ending, bi-level, seventies high-tech "tunnel" architecture—check the bars upstairs, downstairs, the small private foyers (and don't forget the exclusive private club downstairs), and you will be so dizzy that you will be ready for a strong drink. Wait another ten minutes to find a place at the bar and order a $5 drink. Wolf down the ineffectual drink and get ready to boogie. Wait for the "right" music to come on—and you may just wait forever. And if you are really particular about waiting to dance to a recognizable tune, you may as well head home. No Janet Jackson, Whitney Who, or anything hummable. Loud rap, heavy Run DMC beat. Forget Top 40. But besides the music, Tunnel disappoints. Although its knockout interior attracts an interesting crowd night after night, its immense size and the sheer number of people thrown together in one space without any sense of cohesiveness, other than trying to dance to disappointing music, is overwhelming. Welcome the sight of the exit sign and breathe a bit of fresh New York City air. Look a little farther and see the windmills of New Jersey.

21 CLUB
21 West 52nd Street (between Fifth and Sixth Avenues)
☎ 582-7200

Wear the right rep tie and the perfect navy blazer and you might just get greeted with common courtesy when you announce at the door that you are here just for drinks. This club caters to the rich and famous, and most of those folks can afford to drink *and* eat. The place reeks of Brooks Brothers WASPs decked in traditional Ivy League garb. Inhale deeply and you can smell the power and money in the air. Leather chairs and sofas complement a wintry fireplace, front and center. Although the bar is quite long and beautiful, you won't find a single bar stool. You can either have your drinks standing up at the bar or comfort yourself in one of their leather chairs. Order a gin and tonic and fit right in.

23rd STREET BAR & GRILL
158 East 23rd Street (between Lexington and Third Avenues)
☎ 533-8877

I like the East 20s. I like the feel of the neighborhood—
the pretty brownstone blocks, the manicured boutiques,
and the folks who call it home. The young, successful,
mixed crowd lacks the trash and flash of its East Side
neighbors. It is appropriate that the most popular bar in
the neighborhood follows suit and possesses an equally
pleasing personality. No-nonsense, tailored, and looking
like a brightly lit English tavern with striking reds and
greens, the 23rd Street Bar & Grill attracts a becomingly
understated, spirited crowd. Lots of clean-cut, attractive
men in white button-down shirts and yellow ties mix and
mingle with women in sweaters with long straight hair.
The bar is appropriately long and wide; it accommodates
fifteen on bar stools and hosts a generous and comfortable
standing area. Check out the lively after-work scene and
you may wish to stay on for dinner in the rear restaurant.
Style, grace, and tradition ensures 23rd Street Bar & Grill's
continued success. From the looks of it, it's here for some
time to come.

TWENTY TWENTY
20 West 20th Street (between Fifth and Sixth Avenues)
☎ 627-1444

Another hot, trendy little spot (which by publication date
might very well prove to have been a flash in the pan),
this one backed by the team of Ashford & Simpson, is
named for its location: 20 West 20th Street. The doorman,
looking like an extra from *Saturday Night Fever,* greets
you and makes sure you have an easy entrance into this
new addition to Yuppieland. Twenty Twenty's tiered seat-

ing, dark marble floors, slick bar, and overall high-tech look are visually exciting and enticing. After all, its large glass facade certainly makes one curious enough to stare in at the Hollywood-style crowd. Several small tables adjacent to the long bar and alongside the window may induce you to sit down and have a quick drink. Unfortunately, once the camera zooms in for a close-up, blemishes appear. I am sad to report that the blemish of Twenty Twenty rests in the clientele: dowdy patrons trying to look chic, Long Islanders looking New York, and Brooklyn boys sporting gold chains. The crowd here just doesn't cut it. You'll soon be ready to move on. By design, Twenty Twenty is elegant, glamorous, and pretty. Unfortunately, the crowd is none of the above.

TWO ELEVEN BAR & RESTAURANT
211 West Broadway (at Franklin Street)
☎ 925-7202

What was once a local neighborhood haunt where one could go and enjoy an inexpensive, completely forgettable dinner has now gone the way of stylized cuisine—i.e., expensive dining. The room itself—a large, airy, corner room with a trailblazer Tribeca look—hasn't changed substantially. Its soaring minimalist space, with floor-to-ceiling columns, black tin ceiling, overhead fans, hardwood floor, track lighting, and potted palms, is quite attractive. The bar at Two Eleven continues to be an appealing option for casual drinking. In addition to the thirteen-seat S-shaped bar, several small tables and chairs are set up for privacy and for the comfort of relaxing in the company of friends. The crowd at the bar has remained distinctively hip locals and has chosen to pay no heed to the more stylishly attired dinner patrons. Good for chilling out after work, Two Eleven remains delightfully quiet and continues to be a no-nonsense Tribeca mainstay. From the looks of it—here to stay.

UNCLE CHARLIE'S DOWNTOWN
56 Greenwich Avenue (between Perry and Charles Streets)
☎ 255-8787

If you're young, gifted, and gay, own at least five sweaters with a Calvin Klein label, shop at Macy's (or at least date someone from Macy's), and possess a good set of cheekbones, chances are you'll be found imbibing at the downtown bastion of boys: Uncle Charlie's Downtown. This three-barred cruise hall is an eighties delight complete with smoke, mirrors, and video—perhaps the single most popular downtown bar. The clientele are a strictly look-but-don't-touch (let alone talk) crowd. Let's face it—the place has "attitude." The crowd is a mixture of New York LaCoste gay—divorce lawyers, bankers, architects, bakers, and hairdressers—all under forty and all looking for under twenties. The crowd is rarely friendly. Lots of cliques, lots of cruising, very little connecting. The bar enjoys an extremely popular after-work happy hour boasting two drinks for the price of one between the hours of five and eight P.M., making this one of Manhattan's best after-work gay bars. The place is virtually packed at this time of day—probably the best time to investigate this bar, as you get a good mixture of the "suits" and the Levis-and-knapsack set. Otherwise, don't think of going here until at least midnight during the week. At all costs, avoid UCD on weekends unless you're into a heavy suburban and young *crowd* scene. A beer averages $2 but offers you the chance to meet a stranger across a very crowded room. But don't count on it here.

UN DEUX TROIS

123 West 44th Street (between Sixth and Seventh Avenues)

☎ **354-4148**

A lively, spirited, trendy restaurant located in the theater district, with an extremely popular bar frequented by a heavy before- and after-theater crowd. The expanded French-owned restaurant—located in a renovated hotel lobby with structural columns still remaining, tiled floors, and high ceiling—is bright, noisy, fashionable, frenetic, and fun. One of the first restaurants in town to use paper tablecloths and crayons, giving its patrons the chance to doodle and draw through dinner, Un Deux Trois caters not only to the theater crowd, but to the pretty-trendy-people set. Lots of fabulous-looking women dressed in black vogue; many men with French accents, *GQ* ties, long hair, good bone structure, and money. The place has style and so does its clientele. The actual bar, attracting the same crowd as the restaurant, is small—seating maybe ten at the max; but the bar area is SRO late at night, particularly once theater is out. Most come with friends, but the crowd is so closely packed and noisy that it is almost impossible for it *not* to be friendly. Lots of eye-contact games, predominantly straight, but a real blending of sexualities. Un Deux Trois offers trendiness, good food, crowd, and drinks, and a very convenient location. After the curtain comes down on Broadway, the drama begins at Un Deux Trois.

UNION SQUARE CAFE

21 East 16th Street (at Union Square West)

☎ **243-4020**

Union Square Cafe literally shares a wall with its new and trendy next-door neighbor, Metropolis. Apart from this, the two have very little in common. A long, narrow wodden bar runs the length of the entrance into the traditional dining room of Union Square Cafe. It is frequented by an accordingly less flashy and garish crowd than its trendy neighbor. The understated room is warm and inviting, with earthy wood floors, a dark wood bar, and crisp white tablecloths placed on graciously spaced tables. Women in running shoes and business suits unwind with friends here after a tough day at the office. By and large, patrons are upscale and hip, mature and attractive. To help ease the hunger pangs away, the bar serves relishes and other munchies. If you get there early enough, snatch one of the comfortable cocktail tables at the very front. Enjoy the cane chairs and watch the crowd go by your window.

UNITED NATIONS PLAZA HOTEL
First Avenue and 44th Street
☎ 355-3400

Dark and plush, with a decor of sleek black onyx and red upholstered chairs, the UN Plaza bar certainly gets its share of visiting dignitaries, particularly after a hard day at the General Assembly. Located far enough from just about everything else, the UN Plaza bar holds potential for an out-of-the-way romantic tryst. Chances are you will not run into your next-door neighbor (unless of course that's the person you're trysting with). By day, the bar gets a neighborhood-spinster set chatting in all-purpose raincoats and watching visiting dignitaries come and go. The crowd picks up at cocktail time, when a pianist arrives and starts to play Rodgers and Hart melodies. A fine place to rest one's soles after traipsing through the UN with out-of-town guests. Not worth making a special trip unless you are dropping off secret documents to the ambassador of Moldavia.

J.S. VANDAM
150 Varick Street (at VanDam Street)
☎ **929-7466**

What was once a trendy and crowded Tribeca hot spot has now simmered down to a more casual and relaxed establishment. Although its fickle crowd has moved on to the spot of the moment, VanDam's deco bar, with exquisite woodwork, mirrors, and small booths, still merits a visit. Formerly, VanDam's was filled with the late night Tenax set, arriving well after eleven P.M. and staying until the wee hours of the morning enjoying magnums of champagne and checking out the latest fashions. Loud music and sheer number of clients made the bar friendly and easy to meet new friends. Having survived its mid-life crisis, VanDam's has matured gracefully and continues to offer a sophisticated and swank downtown setting where one can be assured of comfort, quiet, and relative privacy. Although there is not much of a crowd remaining at the bar, keep this spot in mind for a cool-down after boogying at nearby S.O.B.'s or Heartbreak.

VAZAC'S
108 Avenue B (at 7th Street)
☎ **473-8840**

An easygoing East Village haunt for over fifty years, Vazac's prides itself on being a neighborhood bar. With its large, dark, horseshoe-shaped bar, ceiling fans, popular jukebox, and inexpensive drinks, Vazac's offers a relaxed and informal spot with mellow bartenders and a friendly crowd. A perfect place to meet your friends to map an evening's strategy. Grab a booth and order beers for $1.50. And to help while away the hours, a video monitor is front and center. A favorite amongst the Hollywood film set; even Paul Newman's *Verdict* drank here.

WALDORF-ASTORIA HOTEL
301 Park Avenue (at 50th Street)
☎ 871-4895

PEACOCK ALLEY. Just one of the several Waldorf-Astoria lobby lounges, Peacock Alley offers lobby drinking amid Manhattan elegance, opulence, and bellhops with underarm stains. In other words, Peacock Alley offers its patrons a mild case of schizophrenia. On the one hand, you are smack in the middle of one of New York's finest hotels, relaxing and drinking out of fine crystal and listening to show tunes being played on a grand piano that once belonged to Cole Porter. On the other hand, you can just as easily focus in on all the hustle and bustle of activity taking place around you. Bellhops are checking in new arrivals faster than they seem to be checking out. If you're quick, you might even catch Mary Tyler Moore making her way to her suite in the towers. But the trick here is to focus in on the piano, toss down a few martinis, and settle back. In no time you'll start to feel like Reno Sweeney.

WARWICK BAR
65 West 54th Street (at Sixth Avenue)
☎ 247-2700
Regardless of the fact that my parents were married here thirty-six years ago, I hold no grudge. But the fact of the

matter is that this corner bar in the Warwick Hotel is a loser. Dark and gloomy, with a requisite wood interior, the Warwick has a bar crowd to match. Although lots of film and TV folk stay at this conveniently located hotel, they certainly seem to avoid the bar. The Warwick attracts a large tourist crowd, which seems to know of no other drinking option in the neighborhood. Although there is plenty of room for privacy, and plenty of munchies served on a hot buffet, cigar smokers, polyester jackets, and out-of-town bouffant hairdos predominate. The dreary crowd adds drabness to this dark pub. Sorry, Mom and Dad, we'll just have to have the anniversary party elsewhere.

WATER CLUB
500 East 30th Street (at the East River)
☎ 683-3333

In a sentence, this is Manhattan's chic and elegant answer to Brooklyn's River Cafe. The upscale and well-heeled WASP set in attendance is evident even before you enter this posh restaurant—just take a look at the lineup of Mercedes, Jaguars, Cadillacs, and limos. Designed and built on a barge on the East River, the Water Club is an elegant spot worth checking out. In winter, you can make yourself at home in the surprisingly traditional, clubby and pubby inside room with its dark green walls dominated by a wonderful blazing fireplace. It's unfortunate that a river view is not available from this room. To really enjoy the Water Club, and to take advantage of its spectacular view, I recommend a spring or summer visit when you can actually sit on the outdoor deck and enjoy the gentle breezes flowing from the East River. Order champagne and pretend you're on the deck of your private yacht. The trick here is to dress and act like you really do own one. Break out the JG Hook and espadrille look. Bon voyage.

WEST END CAFE
2911 Broadway (between 113th and 114th Streets)
☎ 666-8750

This establishment was long a favorite with the Columbia crowd, until the twenty-one-year-old drinking age thinned out the college students to make room for the neighbors. A microcosm of the Upper West Side, the West End is filled with people of all ages: Orientals, blacks, whites, college types (students and professors), and even a punk rocker or two. As you walk in, there's a cafeteria counter serving wholesome food, but the large room is dominated by the huge oval-shaped bar that offers fourteen different brands of beer on tap. Lamps that look like upside-down brandy snifters house electronic candles that illuminate the rafters where glasses hang from wooden racks. The only decorations are the keg heads bearing beer names that hang on the dark wooden walls. A video jukebox plays the latest hits above a few video games and the last remaining pinball machine (remember pinball?). The room is dark and smells a little like beer, but it's seedy in a comfortable way. There's a more open, brighter room in the back with tile floors and brick walls, but it feels a little like a high school cafeteria. For a $6 cover charge you can step into the jazz room where the music's either very cool or very hot, depending on who's playing that night. There's not a bad seat in the intimate room, and the music's always worth the trek to the hinterlands.

WESTFALL
251 East 50th Street (between Second and Third Avenues)
☎ 644-9555

A conveniently located "New York" businessman's bar and grill, Westfall caters to a large East Side contingent.

A long, narrow wooden bar area with exposed brick walls serves as the foyer to the pretty restaurant. The fifteen-seat bar framed by requisite mirror and imitation gas lighting fixtures is known to serve one of the best bacon cheeseburgers in town, appropriately dubbed the Cadillac Burger. The bar does a light lunch business, and many patrons choose to grab a burger and beer right at the bar. Domestic beer runs $2.50. A pretheater menu and a lively after-work crowd create a more convivial atmosphere in the evenings. Most of the patrons tend to be older professionals and dress in business attire. Pretty, basic, and convenient.

WEST 4TH STREET SALOON
174 West 4th Street (between Sixth and Seventh Avenues)
☎ 255-0518

Right on the beaten path, attracting an equally beaten crowd. Recently redone in an attractive wintry, woody style complete with two working fireplaces; West 4th is okay for a pit stop with a friend in the dead of winter when all else fails. If you insist, grab a table far away from the crowd and order a beer and burger. Seating tends to be cramped and uncomfortable, and, whether it is due to the poor architectural acoustics of this place, or just to the rowdy crowd in attendance, you will find yourself in competition with the noise. The crowd is weird—young and tough, with some right out of Washington Square Park. With so many other places in the Village, I can only think of two words, immortalized by Bette Midler in her home video: "Why bother?"

WESTSIDE CAFE
131 West 57th Street (near Eighth Avenue)
☎ **No phone number**

This small French eatery serving moderately priced dinners offers attractive tables ideal for 57th Street sidewalk cruising. Floral wallpaper serves as a pleasant backdrop for large framed French posters, brass fixtures, and a dark wood floor. The room is deceptively large and offers its patrons the option of enjoying the air conditioning in the back of the room on really hot days, or the outside breezes by sitting in the front of the room, near the open doors. The bar doesn't draw much of a crowd, but you'd be hard-pressed to find a more unpretentious, untrendy, hassle-free spot for drinks on this side of town. Nondescript crowd; dress in anything your little heart desires.

THE WHITE HORSE TAVERN
567 Hudson Street (at 11th Street)
☎ **243-9260**

The White Horse, still presiding at its original 1880 location, is one of the oldest Village bars. A popular hangout for poets and writers, it was home to Dylan Thomas. Today, it's popular with a mixture of neighborhood yuppies, old-timers, NYU students, businessmen, and die-hard literary types. With its publike setting, the dark and charmingly dilapidated bar gets a lively after-work crowd. Try a burger and check out the beautiful clock. Perfect to go with friends and catch up on old times. An equally popular outdoor cafe cooks from April through October.

WILSON'S
1441 First Avenue (at 75th Street)
☎ 861-0320

Hanging green plants and a double brass rail separate the dining area from a handsome bar with a brass top and brass siding. Pink globe lights and hanging tulip lamps give a gentle glow to the brick walls. Happy Hour is declared from five till seven P.M., weeknights, and free hors d'oeuvres are available. Tuesday night is ladies' night, with half-priced drinks for women from five till 8:30 P.M. The clientele is mostly middle-aged and consists largely of couples and lone men who gravitate to the bar to gaze at whatever sporting event is rolling across the television screen.

WINDOWS ON THE WORLD
1 World Trade Center
☎ 938-1111

If Cole Porter were to rewrite his song "You're the Top," you can be certain that he would have to add the World Trade Center to his lyric. For it is certainly up there (no pun intended) with the Louvre, the Colosseum, a symphony by Strauss, *and* Mickey Mouse. The tallest building on the East Coast, completed in December 1970, the Trade Center offers unparalleled views of New York. Sharing the 107th floor atop 1 World Trade Center rests the renowned Windows on the World restaurant and its bar mate, the Hors d'Oeuvrerie. While Windows on the World boasts a sumptuous view of midtown Manhattan and its environs, the bar offers a panoramic view of the harbor, Brooklyn, and New Jersey. This is a bar that you cannot afford to miss—whether you are a jaded New Yorker or just here on a visa passing through. Riding up a 747 of an elevator to toast the twinkling lights of the city that never sleeps is something to be experienced.

Management divides the bar area into two spaces. While both are in the same room, the Hors d'Oeuvrerie is the seating section of the bar area for those patrons who wish to enjoy cocktails, hors d'oeuvres, dessert, or coffee at comfortable cocktail tables and chairs. The seating in the room is arranged on multileveled tiers that afford all patrons an equally good view of the harbor. The standing section of the bar, where one can sip, stand, and mingle, is called City Lights. Reservations are not accepted for either spot. The staff is young, professional, and courteous, and deals as adeptly with Aunt Belle from Dayton as with Mr. and Mrs. Donald Trump. Be forewarned— men must wear jackets, and no jeans or denim are allowed in the room—even with the Gloria Vanderbilt name tag.

Apart from intoxicating views, twinkling lights, and starry skies, the elegant atmosphere is enriched even further with entertainment. A pianist and jazz combo that arrives at 7:30 P.M. is guaranteed to get your toes tapping and perhaps seduce you into a quick dance around the floor. Porter, Gershwin, Sondheim, and any other favorites should serve as incentive. Be prepared to spend an additional $2.95 cover charge for music after 7:30 P.M., in addition to an average of $15 for two drinks and perhaps a nibble. Yes—the Hors d'Oeuvrerie is pricey, but how often do you get the opportunity to be Fred and Ginger, with the chance of seeing Halley's Comet shoot right by your very window? And if, baby, you've seen bottom—you'll know this *is* top!

The Hors d'Oeuvrerie is open Monday through Saturday from three P.M. to one A.M.

WINE BAR
422 West Broadway (between Prince and Spring Streets)
☎ 431-4790

A stylish mixture of Soho and Southern California, the Wine Bar specializes in wine by the glass. Over one hundred different types of wine are available for sampling in a relaxed, laid-back, attractive space, sporting white brick walls, a long wooden bar, and many small comfortable tables. The crowd is a mixture of Soho locals, gallery shoppers, and West Broadway tourists. Wine Bar's peaceful setting is fine for sampling wine, reading a gallery guidebook, tasting an appetizer, or meeting a friend for a quiet talk. The staff is knowledgeable and helpful in suggesting a good selection. A curious California "mellow-out" wine-tasting attitude pervades. Like, go with the flow, but leave the alfalfa sprouts at home.

WOODY'S
140 Seventh Avenue South (at Charles Street)
☎ 242-1200

Playing off the glassed-in Seventh Avenue sidewalk cafe concept, Woody's is Charles Street's answer to the Riviera Cafe. Frequented by a more local crowd, Woody's offers a variety of drinking options in a more laid-back atmosphere. You can drink at the dark bar just off the entranceway, sit at any of the tables snaking around the interior, or take a table in the glass-enclosed sidewalk cafe. Weather permitting, you can even grab a table outdoors. It's an ideal spot to visit with friends if some want to eat and others want to drink. You can satisfy both hunger and thirst in an attractive and comfortable surrounding—from early in the morning to late at night. A Village diehard here to stay.

THE WORKS BAR

428 Columbus Avenue (between 80th and 81st Streets)

☎ **799-7365**

Combine uptown preppie and West Side men, add loud music, MTV, porno, attitude, and crowds, and you have the very popular Upper West Side Works. Originally located on 79th Street, the Works has relocated to a space that originally housed an equally popular bar, Cahoots. Cahoots was uptown's answer to Uncle Charlie's Downtown. In other words, you got the young, pretty, "attitude" crowd without having to make the trip all the way downtown. While Cahoots catered to the young bone-structure crowd, the Works courted the Levi 501 men who liked their settings a little darker and seamier. While management has tried to retain the original character and feel of the Works, something was definitely lost when the Works moved into the old Cahoots. The bar is still crotch-to-crotch popular, the crowd is still very much in attendance, the music even continues to be loud, and an occasional porno tape even turns up on Madonna's MTV. But the Works as the old-timers knew it, by trying to assimilate Cahoots, has been left behind somewhere—somewhere in history.

THE WORLD

2nd Street and Avenue C

☎ **477-8677**

Police barricades hold back the anxious young crowd clamoring to get the attention of the equally young door personnel mindlessly choosing which clients shall be admitted. Get selected and stroll right in, or be patient and wait on line; but sooner or later just about everyone gets in. All it seems to take is the ability to fork over the $5 cover charge and look like you're not carrying a concealed weapon. This large two-story space, in a corner of the far East Village (taxi to the door preferable), caters to a young East Village, NYU, and black crowd. Off the stark white entranceway, a staircase leads up to a room which feels like a huge ballroom in a vampire's mansion with peeling red-colored walls and showstopper gothic chandelier. All that's missing are the cobwebs. With small lounges upstairs, religious candles, and proscenium stage, the setting feels like a poor man's Limelight Club. The crowd arrives early and fills the space up quickly; most come with their own dancing partner. Although the East Village crowd is overpowered by the sheer number of blacks, the two are simpatico and the dance floor can get hot. The sound system is incredibly loud and blasts music ranging from sexy and danceable to tuneless and tribal. When your ears need a break, escape to the lounge downstairs and listen to some live entertainment. The most striking feature of this room is the chandelier, which sways ominously from the tumult above. The World provides an inexpensive and large dance space for a young needy crowd. However, don't plan on spending more than eighty minutes (let alone days) around it.

ZIG ZAG
206 West 23rd Street (near Seventh Avenue)
☎ 645-5060

Another new and potentially interesting spot in the middle of Chelsea is this stylish designer bar and bistro. As of this writing, Zig Zag is still being felt out by neighborhood natives, and accordingly its personality is still in the formative stages. The crowd ranges from hip locals to Queens types in for a quick drink. A long, dramatic zigzag bar snakes the length of a narrow brown and bronze windowless room highlighted with fabulous recessed lighting fixtures and enough mirrors to make George Hamilton feel at home. Most of the crowd is here for drinks and draws, including a particularly busy after-work contingent. Perfect for a Perrier before a set at the Midtown Tennis Club.